TIE-DYE

DYE IT, WEAR IT, SHARE IT

SHABD SIMON-ALEXANDER

NEW YORK

Published in the United States by Potter Craft, an imprint of the Crown Publishing Group, a division of Random House, Inc., New York.
www.crownpublishing.com
www.pottercraft.com

POTTER CRAFT and colophon is a registered trademark of Random House, Inc.

Library of Congress Cataloging-in-Publication
Simon-Alexander, Shabd.
Tie-dye: dye it, wear it, share it / Shabd Simon-Alexander.
--First Edition
pages cm
(pbk.)
1. Tie-dyeing. I. Title.
TT853.5.S56 2013
746.6'64--dc23

2012048014

ISBN: 978-0-307-96573-8
eISBN: 978-0-307-96574-5

Printed in the United States of America

Design by Arch & Loop
Still-life photography by Sarah Anne Ward
Photography direction and styling by JoJo Li
Illustrations by JoJo Li
Model and author photography by
Paul Mpagi Sepuya

10 9 8 7 6 5 4 3 2 1

First Edition

CONTENTS

INTRODUCTION

My introduction to tie-dye happened by chance. I was at a garden party where the host had set up an area for tie-dyeing with bottles of brightly colored dye laid out on a picnic table. She gave me a five-minute lesson, and I was hooked. I knotted up old T-shirts and tie-dyed into the night, long after everyone else left. I ended up spending the rest of the summer in that community garden playing with my newfound obsession.

Having studied fine art and photography in school, I was still searching for a distinctive way to express myself, and something about tie-dye really spoke to me. I found it to be the perfect medium with which to experiment and have fun with design. The combination of the planned and the unpredictable is what makes it so enjoyable. I love the surprises that come out of it—many of my favorite results have been happy accidents!

Another thing that makes tie-dye so wonderful is that every piece is truly unique and one-of-a-kind. Patterns can be organic or geometric, colors bold and vibrant or subtle and sophisticated. The possibilities are truly endless.

When I first started tie-dyeing, I searched all over for inspiration and information. I couldn't find anything new, just the same summer-of-love designs I had seen a thousand times before. While I appreciate the role that these patterns played for generations, I knew that tie-dye had potential far beyond what many people might expect. I was determined to see how far I could take this exciting hand-dyeing art. I spent a year exploring its many variations; experimenting with different fabric, color, and pattern combinations. I found inspiration everywhere from marble crosscuts and modern art to the architectural elements on skyscrapers and bridges. One of the things that inspired me the most were pictures of space from NASA's Hubble Space Telescope. I used these images of farway nebulas as the inspiration to create a design for a pair of leggings. I got such a great response every time I wore them that I decided to start a small line of hand-dyed jersey basics. Over the years, my dye project developed into a full-fledged fashion line that is now found in boutiques all over the world.

People had such a positive response, not only to the clothing itself, but also to the fact that my pieces are made by hand. And what's more, they were thrilled by the idea that they could make something similar themselves. I realized that I didn't want to keep the knowledge I had gained to myself so I began to share it in workshops and classes.

I love the look on people's faces as they see their creations come to life. Tie-dye is virtually impossible to do incorrectly, so it is the perfect artistic project for those of us with more enthusiasm than technical skill. It is easy to learn, and open to interpretation to suit your own personal style. The more you experiment with it, the more you'll see that just by tweaking one simple element, you can achieve vastly different results. Exploring these endless possibilities is what makes tie-dye so addictive.

My love for tie-dye has grown madly over the years, and I have found teaching it so rewarding that I want to share it with a wider audience. In this book, I reveal all of my secrets to you, and I hope to inspire you to share my love of dyeing and to have fun!

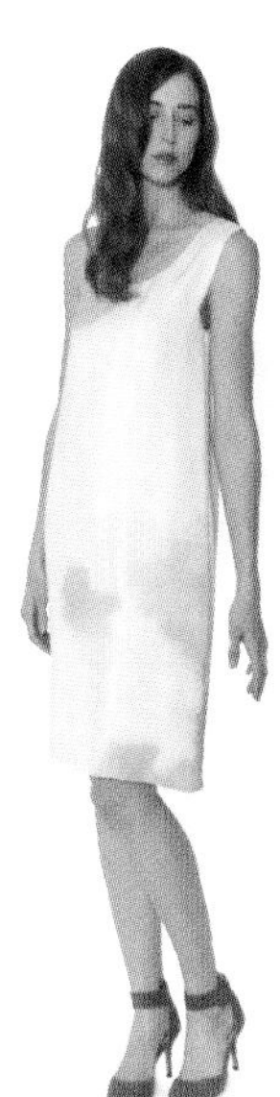

HOW TO USE THIS BOOK

In the first part of this book, I give you a little background on what tie-dye is and how you do it. This section is packed with information on how to set up your work area and what materials you need, and provides a step-by-step overview of the basic dyeing process. It will be helpful to read this section before you begin dyeing, as the projects later on will refer back to it. Readers who are ready to tackle more advanced dyeing will also find some color theory and design concepts to help guide creative choices.

In the second part of the book, I'll show you some of my favorite project ideas. I know some of you will want to move straight to this section. These projects feature different tying methods so you can see how simple changes can create interesting new patterns. I've rated the projects by difficulty, from beginner-friendly to advanced. There are also several projects, including the Lightning Tee (page 72), the Crystalline Scarf (page 84), and the Indigo Button-Down (page 117), that are especially quick and easy. I have included the curing time for each project, but please keep in mind that for most dyeing projects you should allow at least an hour for the rest of the process, including setup, dyeing, and cleanup. In the interest of streamlining the instructions, I've also included a cheat sheet at the back of the book. Copy this and use it while you dye.

While I provide all of the information that you need for each project, I encourage you to simplify when possible, experiment, and generally enjoy the process. I note the colors I used for each of the samples photographed, but feel free to choose your own—that's one of the best parts of dyeing things yourself! Experiment with mixing techniques; try a tying method from one project with the dyeing process of another. Use the lessons in this book as a jumping-off point, and remember there is no wrong way to tie-dye. The possibilities are endless; go play!

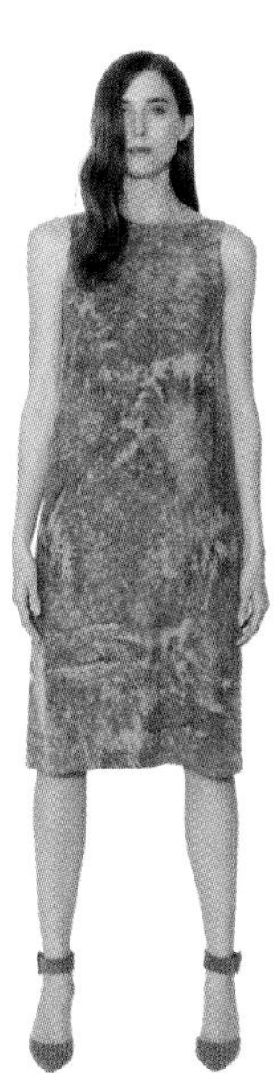

ALL ABOUT TIE-DYE

I love tie-dye. I love how it looks; I love making it; and I also love the story that it tells. By looking at beautiful dyed textiles and clothing, we can learn some of the secrets perfected by the generations of artists and craftspeople who came before us. The art of tie-dye has been around for nearly two thousand years, and its history is filled with intriguing stories of travel, trade, religion, and culture from ancient times through to Woodstock and the present day. Today, the tradition of tie-dye is alive and well and practiced throughout the world, with established techniques serving as the foundation for the innovative designs seen everywhere from rural villages to high-fashion runways.

Tie-dye has been reinvented by every generation to use it. The designs are influenced by the people creating them, their culture, and the changing times. I kept traditional techniques in mind while designing the projects for this book. But instead of being direct references, the projects are all updated, contemporary designs with historical roots.

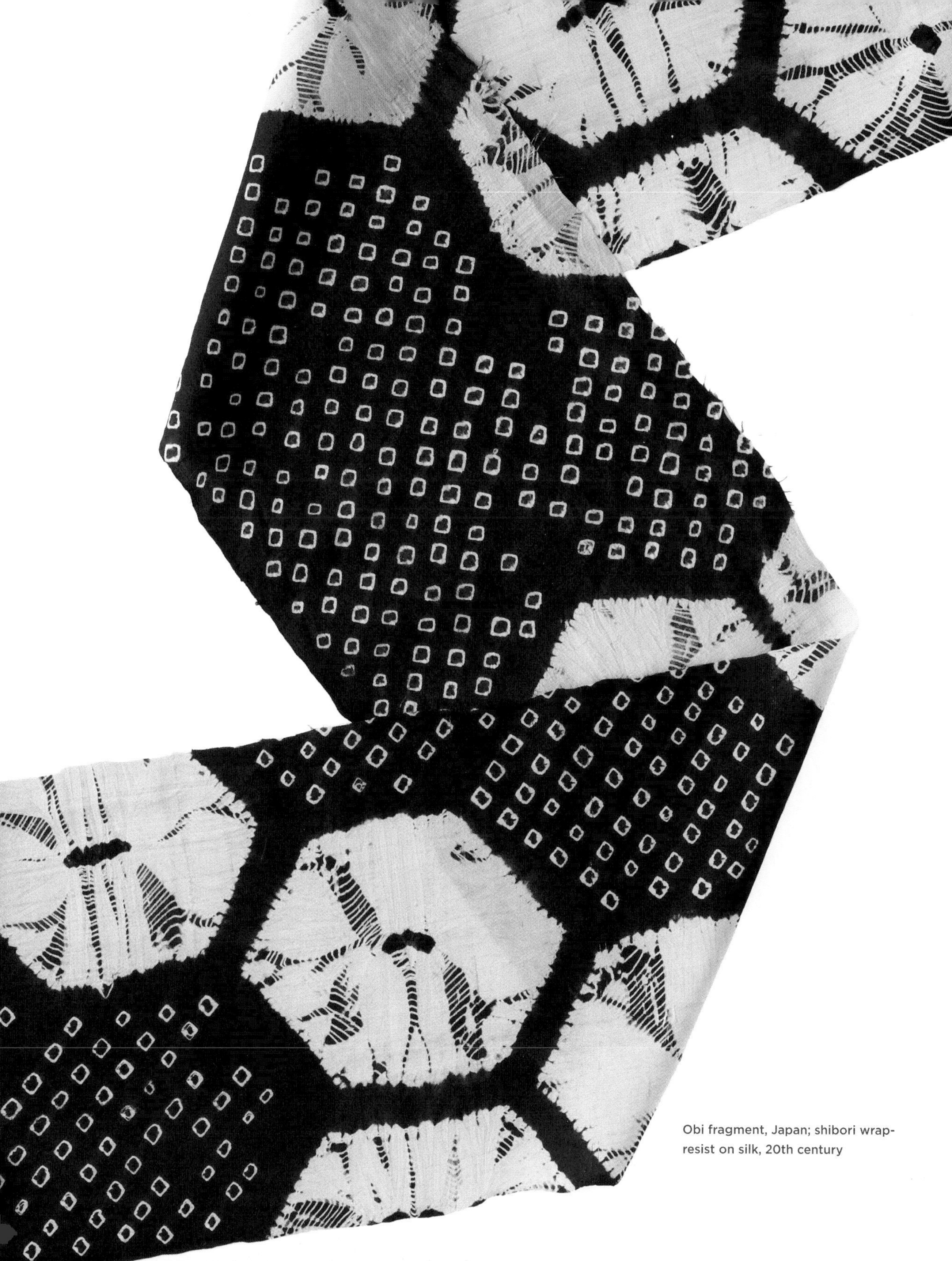

Obi fragment, Japan; shibori wrap-resist on silk, 20th century

THE ART OF DYEING

Dyeing is such an ancient art that we don't even know when it began, but records indicate that it has been practiced throughout the world for more than six thousand years. The desire for vibrantly colored textiles gave rise to ancient trade routes throughout the Middle East, and led to the establishment of the Silk Road connecting to the Far East. When the Spanish first arrived in the Americas, they were amazed by the bright red hue that the Aztec and Maya peoples developed using the cochineal insect, and they quickly established a valuable export trade, second only to silver. So it is no wonder that dye techniques were once considered heavily guarded secrets!

In medieval Europe, apprentices would study for years under a dye master with a secret book of recipes before earning the possibility of being invited into the guild themselves. In Central Asia, different ethnic groups held the secrets to dyeing different colors; and the threads for a single robe would pass through the hands of Tadjik dyers to create the yellow and red sections, and then to Jewish dyers for the complex indigo blue, before being woven together into a complicated and stunning design.

TIE-DYE AROUND THE WORLD

Tie-dye, known as *shibori* in Japan, *plangi* in Indonesia, *bandhani* in India, and *adire* in West Africa, includes any technique in which fabric is gathered, folded, twisted, rolled, tied, stitched, or bound to resist the application of dye. It is one of the oldest and most prevalent resist-dyeing techniques. The other major resist-dye techniques are *ikat*, in which the threads are bound and dyed before being woven into cloth, and *batik*, in which the fabric is drawn on or stamped with wax or a resist paste before being dyed.

Tie-dye is a democratic medium; it has been made and worn by the elite as a demonstration of their wealth, and by the poor to refresh simple, worn-out clothing. Patterns vary from detailed and refined to bold and dramatic, and include geometric, floral, and figurative designs, depending on the culture and personal preference. Active production continues worldwide, most notably in Africa, Japan, western India, and southern China. Today, tie-dye—rather unfairly stereotyped as a sixties trend—is enjoying a resurgence of popularity, with designers pushing the boundaries of classic traditions in new and innovative ways.

Turban, Jaipur, Rajasthan, India; leheria wrap-resist on cotton, c. 1860s

ASIA Asian textile traditions are rich in history and variety, and encompass weaving, embroidery, rug making, ikat, batik, and tie-dyeing. Tie-dye examples from all over Asia tend to reflect the aesthetic of the other textiles in each region. The tie-dyes of Uzbekistan and Central Asia share the bright, bold coloring of local ikat designs. Similarities are also found crossing borders. The dye patterns from the Hill tribe of Thailand are reminiscent of those in southwestern China. Tie-dyed fabrics made by the Islamic people of Cambodia and the Philippines are related to those made by Indonesian and Indian Muslims. Circle-adorned woolen fabrics are found throughout the Himalayan regions of Tibet and India as well as in the cold regions of Mongolia. These examples show how traditions have often traveled with minority groups, sharing their knowledge and keeping their customs alive.

CHINA Some of the oldest examples of tie-dye seem to be of Chinese origin. Thought to have originated around 2000 years ago in either the Qin or Han Dynasties, ancient Chinese tie-dyes, often complex and pictorial, were once prized and popular artworks. Pieces dating from the fifth to the sixth century AD have been found along trade routes as far away as Egypt and Turkistan. Even the oldest *shibori* pieces found in Japan seem to be Chinese imports. Over the years, other forms of textile works, such as complex weavings, overtook the popularity of tie-dye in China, and today *zha ran* ("tie dye") is only produced in a few parts of the Szechuan and Yunnan provinces.

JAPAN *Shibori* (literally meaning "wring, squeeze, press") encompasses many variations, and is among the most recognized forms of tie-dye. Although Japanese *shibori* fabric may be dyed in a rainbow of colors, the most well known is the deep, rich indigo. Originally used by the poor to cheaply decorate old cotton and hemp clothing, the technique was later used for the elegant silk clothing of the upper classes as well. Apprentices study under a master for as long as ten years to learn the trade, a highly regarded craft. There are over two hundred recognizable patterns, many of which can be traced back to individual artists. Shibori is ever evolving; contemporary Japanese designers continue to develop methods to incorporate the new technologies and high-tech materials available today.

INDIA The Ajanta cave drawings in India depict some of the world's oldest records of tie-dye. The trade is still practiced today, mainly in Gujarat and Rajasthan, and tie-dye continues to be worn by people of all castes. Tie-dye in India is often made by Muslims, with the women doing the tying and the men the dyeing. Designs can range from simple stripes to complex geometric patterns and elaborate scenes depicting animals, plants, and people. The most common technique, known as *bandhani* ("to tie"), was the

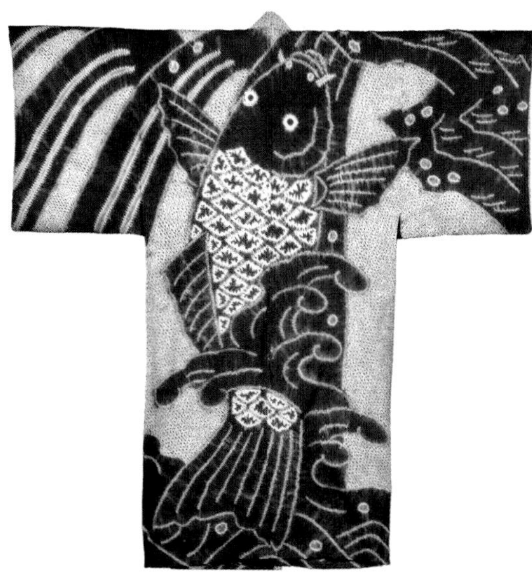

Kimono, Tohoko, Japan; indigo-dyed shibori stitch- and wrap-resist on cotton, 19th/early 20th century

original inspiration for the American bandana. The fabric is tied by women and girls who grow their nails long or wear spiked metal rings to pinch bits of cloth for patterns that incorporate countless circles. *Leheria* ("wave") is another process in which the fabric is folded, rolled, tied and then dyed to create stripes and complex zigzag patterns. Colors tend to be bright, and designs are often tied and dyed multiple times before being finished—a complicated design can take up to four months to complete, and ties are often left on the fabrics when they are sold in order to prove authenticity.

INDONESIA Tie-dye was believed to have traveled to Indonesia centuries ago through trade with India, and the geometric forms may have been particularly enticing to the Islamic people of Indonesia, whose laws prohibited the representation of organic forms. *Plangi* ("rainbow") is a process in which fabric is folded, rolled, or tied, sometimes with shells or rocks inside, to create intricate relief patterns. *Tritik* ("drops of water") is another method in which oversized geometric designs are stitched into the cloth, leaving behind trails of dotted lines reminiscent of small drops of water. Like the Indian traditions, fabric is often folded, tied, and dyed multiple times to create colorful, repeated patterns. Other textile arts renowned in the area, such as batik and ikat, are close relatives of tie-dye.

MIDDLE EAST AND NORTH AFRICA The tie-dyes of North Africa and the Middle East are some of the most striking examples, often incorporating a free-form, artistic nature unique to the region. These pieces, often in wool, are generally simple in design and dyed in rich, earthy colors. Stunning examples of dresses, head scarves, and face veils can be found in Syria and Yemen, but perhaps the most noteworthy are the textiles

Lawon ritual shoulder cloth, Palambang, Sumatra, Indonesia; tritik stitch-resist with mixed dyes on silk, 19th century

Assaba woman's head wrapper, Berber, Dahar Mountains, Tunisia; wool, sprang- and shaped-resist, first half 20th century

of the Berber peoples in Morocco and Tunisia. Women's veils from Morocco are sometimes tied with circle motifs, but may also include minimalistic dip-dyed color blocking or detailed hand-painted henna designs. Veils from Tunisia are often dyed by women in modern, asymmetrical patterns, and then embroidered by men. Others are made with intricate designs woven directly into the woolen scarves in cotton; when dyed, the design appears in relief, as only the wool absorbs the color.

AFRICA The variations of tie-dye in Africa are as numerous and diverse as the continent is vast, and tie-dyed fabric is still produced all over Africa today, for both personal use and export internationally. West Africa is especially well known for its tie-dyes, which vary from region to region and are sometimes referred to by the Yoruba term *adire* ("tie and dye"). In Nigeria, hand-stitched designs are made by women, with similar machine-stitched designs made by men. After they are dyed a deep indigo, pieces of the raffia used in the hand stitching are left in the fabric to prove authenticity. Related techniques are practiced in Cameroon as well as by the Soninke and Wolof people of Senegal. The Kuba people of Congo and Dida people of Ivory Coast tie and bind raffia cloth before dyeing it in earthy brown hues. Fabrics from The Gambia are commonly scrunched to create marbled patterns in a rainbow of colors. Africa has had a particularly international relationship when it comes to tie-dye, seamlessly merging foreign techniques and aesthetics with its own, and in turn introducing them to people all over the world. Some even say that the tie-dyes from the Hausa region, brought back to the United States by Peace Corps volunteers, were the inspiration for the tie-dyes popularized in America in the 1960s.

EUROPE The history of resist-dyeing in Europe is largely one of trade and industrialization, but the role Europe played in popularizing resist-dyeing techniques throughout the world cannot be overlooked. Between the sixteenth and nineteenth centuries, the Dutch played a major role in importing batik fabric from India and Indonesia. These imports inspired home-grown production of wax-dye prints, both on the industrial level in Holland and England, and in countless family-owned *Blaudruck* ("blue print") workshops throughout central and western Europe. Silk resist painting, brought over with the Russian aristocracy who fled the Bolshevik Revolution, became popular in French haute couture in the 1920s. Ikat was also produced throughout Europe, inspired by Italian imports from the Middle East and Russian imports from Central Asia. Fabrics using true tie-and-dye techniques in Europe are rare, confined to a few nineteenth-century examples in Sweden and Hungary. Perhaps this is why in many European countries today they still use the word *batik* as a catchall term for any resist-dyed fabric.

(Top row, left to right) Turban, India; futon cover, Japan; woman's shoulder cloth, Indonesia. (2nd row, left to right) Shoulder scarf, Morocco; woman's veil, Morocco; ritual cloth, Cameroon. (3rd row, left to right) Woman's dowry cloth, Ivory Coast; festival banner, Central Asia; woman's ceremonial veil, Morocco. (4th row, left to right) Ritual shoulder cloth, Indonesia; ritual cloth, Ivory Coast; horse blanket, Tibet. See page 157 for additional information.

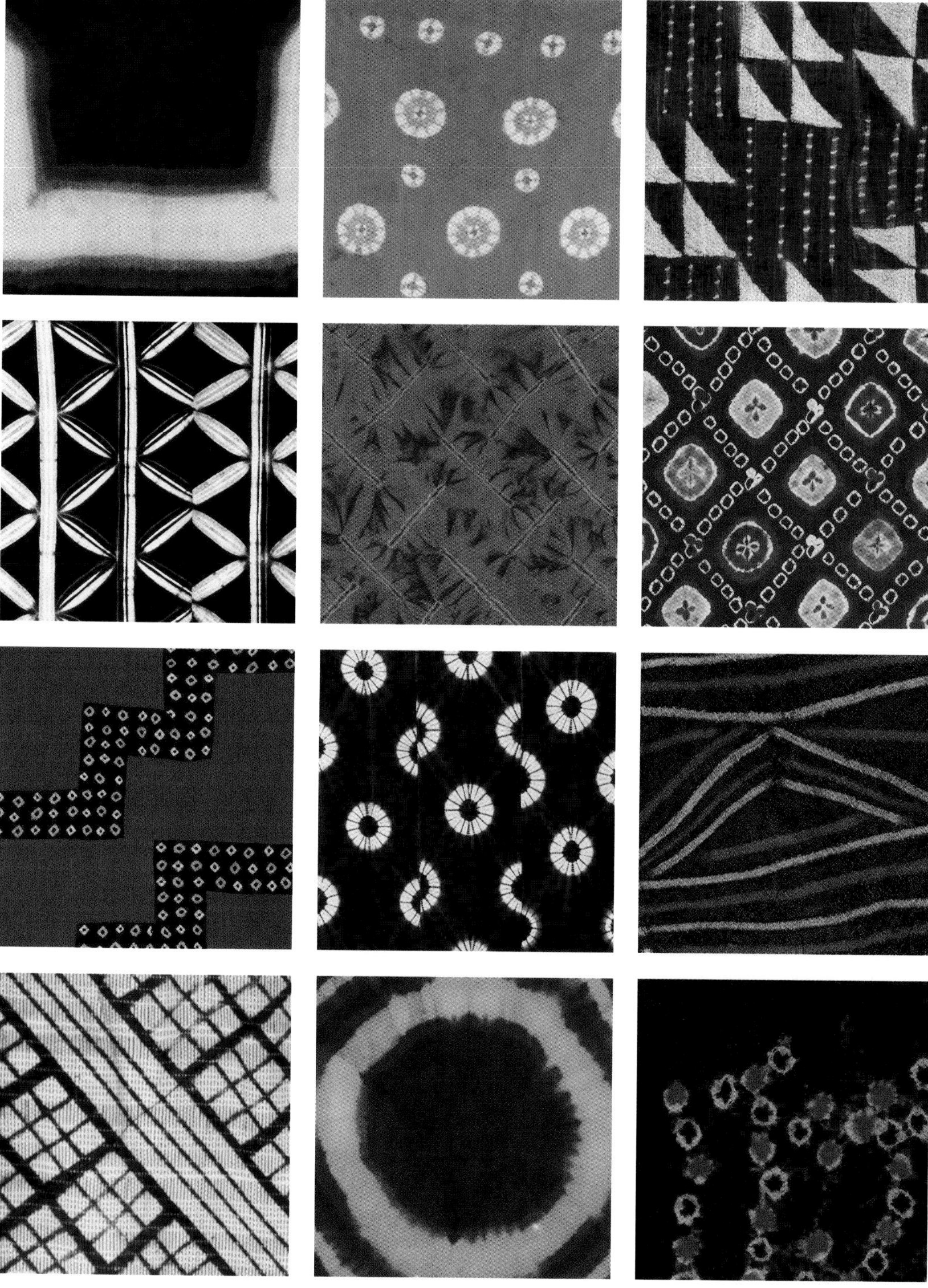

(Top row, left to right) Woman's ceremonial veil, Morocco; tea ceremony cloth, Mongolia for the Japanese market; Ukara cloth, Nigeria. (2nd row, left to right) Ukara cloth, Nigeria; man's ceremonial skirt, Congo; banner, Indonesia. (3rd row, left to right) Mantle, Peru; futon cover, Japan; ritual emblem of a chief, Ivory Coast. (4th row, left to right) Woman's summer kimono, Japan; scarf, Morocco; head shawl, Tunisia. See page 157 for additional information.

SOUTH AMERICA Some of the oldest tie-dyed fabrics have been discovered throughout South America, in present-day Peru, Chile, Argentina, and Bolivia. Called *amarra* ("to tie"), these pre-Hispanic artifacts included designs that were utilized almost like language, with different elements—polychrome and colorful, geometric and figurative—telling stories. Separate pieces of woolen fabric would sometimes be tie-dyed in different colors and then joined together to form one large patchwork with a continuous design. Other examples include designs that continue into the fringe of woven fabrics, a technique rarely seen elsewhere. The repression of indigenous populations during the Spanish colonization of South America led to the near extinction of this craft, but renewed interest in recent years has led to the study of *amarra* as a historically important art form.

MESOAMERICA In the travel notebooks of Spanish conquistadors, there are repeated references to the tie-dyed cloaks of Aztec emperors decorated in symbolically significant square, diamond, and circle patterns. They are believed to have been made using both tlalpilli (Nahuatl for "tied or knotted") and batik techniques, and dyed in indigo. Evidence also shows that influence from early Mexican tie-dyes traveled as far north as Arizona. Tie-dyeing is no longer common in contemporary Mexico or Central America; however, double-weave ikats from Guatemala and Mexico are still prized today for the complex designs dyed and woven into them.

UNITED STATES You might be surprised to learn that tie-dye has been practiced in America since the early 1900s. Women used it to make quilt fabrics, to replicate the painted-silk French fashions popular in the 1920s, and to decorate inexpensive feed-sack dresses during the Great Depression. During the 1950s, synthetic dyes and cold-water fiber-reactive dyes allowed for the bright colors that eventually became synonymous with the hippie movement and a generation's need to express its individuality. In a clever business move, Rit dye approached artists, encouraging them to experiment with tie-dye in the hopes of popularizing the technique and creating a new market for their dyes. They sponsored vendors at Woodstock and gave tie-dyed shirts to performers, and history was made. Fashion designers such as Halston soon adopted the trend, celebrities began to wear tie-dye, and the mainstream followed. Now a summer camp standard, tie-dye has also enjoyed continued experimentation among textile artists and a recent resurgence as both a craft medium and a high-fashion statement.

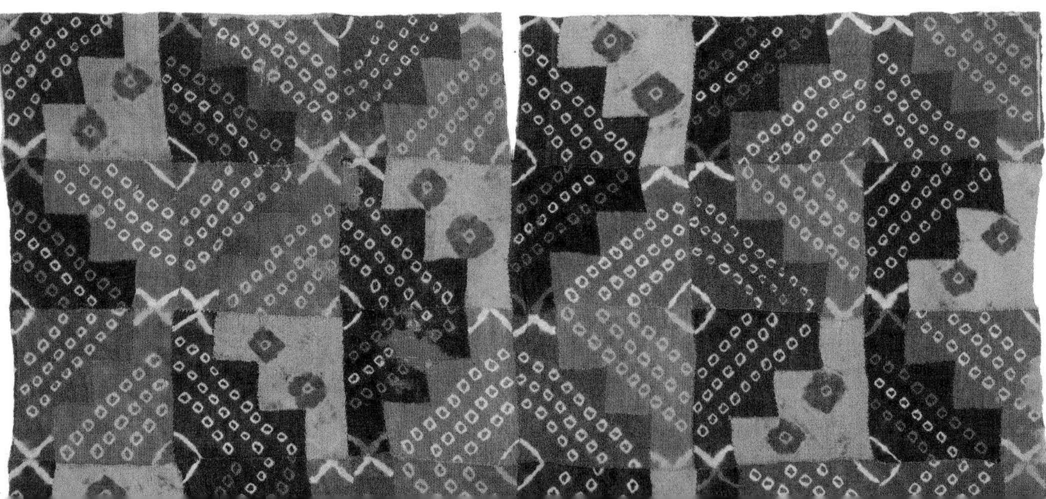

Huari piecework tunic, Huari culture, Peru; amarra wrap-resist with natural dyes on camelid hair, 750–950 AD

TIMELINE

15,000 BC	Natural pigments used as cosmetics, to decorate belongings, and in cave paintings, such as those discovered in Lascaux and Altimira.
6000+ BC	Earliest textiles found in Anatolia (present-day Turkey), Egypt, and Palestine.
4000-3000 BC	Dyeing becomes an established craft in India, China, and South America.
2000 BC	Trade of dyed silk fabric throughout the Middle East.
327 BC	"Beautiful printed cottons" in India mentioned by Alexander the Great.
200 BC-AD 200	Earliest records of Chinese tie-dye from the Qin or Han Dynasties.
100 BC	Silk Road establishes textile trade from China and the Far East to Europe and Africa.
AD 400-500	Earliest examples of Chinese tie-dye found in Egypt and the Middle East.
400-600	Earliest record of Indian resist-dye found in the Ajanta cave drawings in India depict resist-dyed clothing.
500-800	Earliest examples of pre-Hispanic tie-dye found in Peru.
600-800	Japan learns *shibori* from China.
1400s	Sea routes and trade established to bring dyestuffs from the Americas and Asia to Europe.
1500s	Europeans, notably the Spanish and Portuguese, followed by the Dutch, British, and French, begin importing resist-dyed fabrics from India and Indonesia.
1700s-1800s	The Dutch begin a wax-resist textile industry in Holland with export to Indonesia and Africa; other home-grown wax-resist industries spring up all over central Europe for local sale.
1856	William Henry Perkins develops the first synthetic dye (in England), called mauveine or aniline purple.
EARLY 1900s	Tie-dyeing becomes known in the United States.
1954-1956	Fiber-reactive dyes are invented and become commercially available.
LATE 1950s-1960s	Tie-dye takes off in the United States.

MATERIALS

One of the best things about tie-dye is how easy and cheap it is to begin. You don't need to invest in a lot of tools or have a dedicated space; in fact, it really requires just four basics: fabric, dye, water, and soda ash, which bonds the dye to the fabric. However, you can add a multitude of other tools to your arsenal depending on your interest and needs. Many supplies can be found secondhand or at your local hardware, kitchen supply, or dollar store. You might even have the tools lying around the house already—just make sure that once you use them for dyeing, you use them *only* for dyeing!

SETTING UP

Before you start, set up your space so you—and your house—stay clean. As long as you have a flat surface (a table or floor) and you cover it to keep it clean, you can really dye anywhere. A plastic tarp and old newspapers are an inexpensive way to keep your area protected and allow for easy cleanup at the end. Keep a stack of old rags, dish towels, or paper towels around for wiping your hands, drying your tools, and cleaning up spills. I also recommend that you wear an apron or old clothes while working (the same dyes that are dyeing your fabrics will permanently dye anything you're wearing too!). Make sure you have access to a water source, both for mixing your dyes and chemicals and for washing things at the end. That said, when I used to tie-dye in the community garden, I would leave my presoak solution there, covered and ready to reuse, and I would bring everything home in plastic bags to wash, so I really didn't need water while I was there.

Although tie-dye is a relatively safe and nontoxic medium, there are some general, commonsense guidelines to follow (see the sidebar, "Safety First"). It's always a good idea to use rubber gloves whenever handling dye (you can buy the medical kind at any pharmacy, or sturdier ones from a dye supplier) and to wear a dust mask when mixing dye powder or other chemicals. Also, because dye can stain anything it comes in contact with, rinse out your sink or tub right away if you've used it to wash your supplies and projects.

SAFETY FIRST

Work in a well-ventilated area.

Use gloves, an apron, a dust mask, and eye protection whenever necessary. All fine powders are potentially harmful if breathed in.

Keep a set of tools solely for dyeing, clearly labeled and separate from your kitchen items. Never use the same tools for preparing, eating, or storing food.

Always supervise children (and animals) around chemicals.

Store all dyes and chemicals in clearly labeled containers and keep them in a cool dark place. (If you need to store dyes or chemicals in the fridge, seal the container well and label it clearly.)

Dispose of all dyes and chemicals as instructed on the labels; they can generally be disposed of as you would any washing liquid.

If you experience an adverse reaction to any product, stop using it and consult a doctor.

GENERAL TOOLS

The exact tools needed differ slightly for different dyeing methods, such as immersion dyeing and direct application, and vary even more depending on the project. I outline below the general tools needed for a fully stocked tie-dye studio, but check the materials list for individual projects to see which tools are necessary for the projects you plan on trying first; then collect the remainder of the tools as you need them.

BUCKETS Buckets are the multitasker of the dye work space. You can use them for mixing dyes and chemicals, immersing your projects in a dye bath, storing your garments as they cure, and carrying water to your work space. I like to save yogurt and take-out containers to use as smaller buckets, and have a few buckets in 1-, 2-, and 5-gallon sizes for larger projects.

MIXING TOOLS Buy a dedicated set of tools for mixing dyes and chemicals. Measuring cups, measuring spoons, funnels, and a whisk, spoon, or something else to stir with are all things you'll need. Keep them well labeled and separate from the tools you use in your kitchen.

OLD NEWSPAPERS Lay down old newspapers to help soak up excess dye so it doesn't pool under your project or run off the sides of the table. Use newspapers that are at least a month old as the ink isn't likely to transfer. If you intend to do a lot of dyeing, you can also set up a shallow container with a grate over it to catch the excess dye instead of using newspapers.

PLASTIC BAGS You need to keep your fabric wet to let the color set. Resealable plastic storage bags, grocery bags, plastic wrap, and tarps are all great for this— you can use anything that will keep your garment wet during the curing process.

STORAGE CONTAINERS Some dyes and chemicals can be saved and reused for later projects. You can store them in resealable containers like milk jugs, plastic storage containers, or squeeze bottles.

PLASTIC SQUEEZE BOTTLES It's best to mix your dyes in plastic bottles (the kinds used for hair dye or ketchup). They allow you to apply dyes onto fabric easily, and to store extra dye for later use.

RUBBER BANDS AND STRING I keep a variety of rubber bands of different sizes and thicknesses for tying a range of fabrics. String, twine, floss, or waxed thread can also be used.

OPTIONAL DESIGN TOOLS Several projects in this book explore designs made with more unusual items. Marbles, rocks, beans, or rice can be used to create small circular patterns. Clamps and pieces of wood or plastic can be used to create relief shapes. Plastic tubing is sometimes used to wrap fabric for certain *shibori* dye methods, as are a needle and thread. Chalk, pencils, or a water-soluble fabric marker can help you plot your design before starting. Paintbrushes or sponges can be used to paint directly onto fabric with the dye. You can also try a variety of other types of tools, such as spray bottles, forks, syringes—anything that will let you apply the dye directly to the fabric in a new and exciting way.

WHITE WAR
100% PURE BRISTLE MADE IN INDONESIA
decopatch
SPORTS BRIEFING
TENNIS
Bryan Brothers Keep U.S. Alive

DYES AND ADDITIVES

The dyes and additives used in this book are available at most art-supply and craft stores as well as through online retailers. They are non-toxic and kid-friendly, and ideal for both home and professional use.

Over the years, innovations in the dye industry have brought about dyes for all types of uses. The invention of Procion cold-water fiber-reactive dyes in 1956 revolutionized the dye process, allowing people to apply a variety of colors directly to fabrics without the use of boiling water. These versatile dyes offered a previously unknown lasting quality and did not fade in light or after washing. They are the most common dyes used for industrial, professional, hobby, and home use, and their introduction allowed for the boom of contemporary tie-dye, batik, and fabric painting.

The techniques in this book can also be used with a variety of other types of dyes for different effects. Various dyes exist for specific uses on silks and synthetics. Natural dyes have also had a recent resurgence with home dyers, crafters, and artists, and continue to be used by some indigenous groups throughout the world. For a listing of different dyes and their advantages and limitations, refer to the chart on pages 152–153.

FIBER-REACTIVE DYES In this book, I work exclusively with cold-water fiber-reactive dyes, also known as Procion MX dyes. While you can use the techniques in this book with most types of dyes, and are welcome to do so, I find that fiber-reactive dyes are hands down the best, most versatile dyes, and they're always what I recommend for multicolored projects. With fiber-reactive dyes you don't need a stove, hot water, or any fancy equipment. Plus they're permanent and fade resistant, and they yield rich, vibrant colors. You can buy hundreds of premade colors from manufacturers such as Dharma Trading, Jacquard, or PRO Chemical & Dye, or start with primary colors and mix your own (for more on color mixing, see page 40).

Mixed dyes start to slowly lose their strength after a few hours, but if you aren't concerned with getting consistent results, they can be stored in a cool dark space and reused for weeks. If you mix soda ash with them, however, they will completely lose their strength after a few hours and can't be reused.

THE SCIENCE BEHIND THE ART

In high school I tried to convince my teachers that I didn't need to study math and science because I was going to be an artist and designer. It turns out I was right about what I was going to do, but totally wrong about the math and science part! I use math every day to calculate proportions and figure out dye formulas. My studio is basically a chem lab! My favorite parts of my work are the "science experiments" I conduct when trying out new techniques and colors.

Unlike paints, where the color sits on top of fabric, dyes actually become a part of the fibers themselves. Fiber-reactive dyes will work on any natural fiber; they are made for use on plant-based fabrics like cotton and linen, but also work on silk and wool, and even wood and paper. Soda ash raises the pH level of the fabric and prepares it to accept fiber-reactive dyes, which then form a permanent molecular bond with the fibers. Each color has its own dye molecule with a unique shape, which causes it to reflect and absorb light differently. This is how color is created.

In immersion dyeing (page 60), salt can be used to help push the dye molecules out of the water and into the fabric, making more intense colors. The soda ash used in tie-dye causes dyes to bond with water molecules as well, leaving less dye available to bond with fabric fibers, so the dye begins to lose strength if mixed with soda ash.

The dye process continues for up to twenty-four hours, after which all of the possible bonds have been made and any excess dye molecules can be washed away, with the rest becoming permanent.

SODA ASH FIXER One of the nice things about working with fiber-reactive dyes is that you can use soda ash as a universal fixative with all colors (unlike dyeing with natural dyes, in which different fixatives, or mordants, are needed for different colors). Soda ash, also known as sodium carbonate Na_2CO_3, is a mild alkali that raises the pH level of fabric and allows fiber-reactive dyes to create a permanent bond with the fiber molecules. It's nontoxic and has a wide variety of other uses. Sodium carbonate has been used in glass manufacturing, photography, and taxidermy as well as in products made for eco-friendly household cleaning and for dechlorinating pools; however, always wear gloves when you handle it, as soda ash can be a little rough on the skin.

Soda ash and dyes need to work together on the fabric, but the order of application can differ depending on the process you are using. The soda ash can be used as a presoak before the dye (as in most tie-dye), mixed directly in with the dye (when used for painting), or mixed in after the dye (as recommended for standard immersion dyeing).

ALTERNATIVE *If you have very sensitive skin you can use its cousin, baking soda. The process required tends to be more messy and time consuming, and results are less vibrant and permanent. Because baking soda is a weaker alkali than soda ash, you will need to add heat, by boiling the fabric in water and baking soda for an hour before dyeing, or by microwaving it for ten minutes either before or after applying the dye. Aside from the addition of heat, you can use the same calculations and instructions as for dyeing with soda ash (see pages 50 to 67). Please be careful when working with hot water.*

If stored in a tightly covered container so it doesn't evaporate, a soda ash mixture without any dye in it can be kept and reused indefinitely.

DETERGENT When washing out your tie-dye the first time, the best results are achieved by using a specialized laundry detergent called Synthrapol (available wherever fiber-reactive dyes are sold). Synthrapol prevents the dye from redepositing on the fabric as you wash it out, keeping the colors vibrant and distinct.

ALTERNATIVE *Similar results can be achieved using a delicate dishwashing liquid; the same thing that keeps the grease from sticking to your dishes as you wash them will keep the dye from muddying up your clothes. I generally like to use eco-friendly laundry detergents, which also work because they are free of harsh chemicals that react poorly with the dye (no bleach, please!).*

OPTIONAL ADDITIVES To help speed things along, I like to use as few elements as possible in my process, but the following optional additives might come in handy for specific projects.

UREA helps dye dissolve better in water. It makes mixing easier, and it reduces the likelihood of getting explosions of undissolved dye particles on your finished piece. It will also keep your garment moist longer, which can be useful when attempting projects such as fabric painting, where you want the fabric to remain wet.

SODIUM ALGINATE is a natural product made from seaweed that can be used to thicken dye for use in direct painting or silk screening. It's nice because it won't add texture to the fabric the way that paint does.

SALT You can also mix common noniodized household salt directly in with immersion dye baths to help create more intensity in darker tones. Rock salt can create interesting effects when sprinkled on top of dyed garments while still wet.

CALSOLENE OIL is a wetting agent that helps to spread dye evenly in the water. It is especially helpful when trying to create smooth ombré effects.

WATER SOFTENER is useful if you live in an area with hard water, which can interfere with the dyeing process.

REDURAN HAND CLEANER works like magic if your hands somehow become covered in dye.

THINGS TO KNOW WHEN SHOPPING FOR DYE

A variety of companies sell fiber-reactive dyes, and while each brand has its own range of colors, the basic chemical makeup is the same, so different dyes can be used together. I tend to buy from different companies depending on which colors I prefer. I also mix these colors together to make my own. Keep in mind that each company has its own secret formulas for its colors, so the name "coral" might refer to pink in one brand and orange in another. Also, the color as it appears in powder form does not necessarily represent the actual color results on fabric. Most brands can provide fabric or printed color swatches that are more accurate (keeping all of the possible variables like quantity, dye method, and fabric in mind, of course; see page 65).

There are also fiber-reactive dyes with the fixative already included. Jacquard offers iDye, premixed packages that can be used in a washing machine or heated in a large stockpot on the stove. Tulip offers One-Step, bottles of dye premixed with baking soda (sodium bicarbonate, the weaker cousin of soda ash). These both offer a quick, simple dyeing process, but are less versatile. The results also may be less vibrant and permanent than the results achieved by using fiber-reactive dyes in the ways outlined in this book.

Dye additives can generally be found wherever you buy your dye. Since soda ash serves so many other uses, it can also be found at pool supply stores and some hardware stores, labeled as sodium carbonate.

GETTING TO KNOW FABRICS

It is important to understand your fabrics in order to choose the right one for each project. I'll outline a few differences in the way the dye takes to each fiber, but remember that you need to consider the washability of your fabric as well. For example, while wool will accept the dye, if you wash it in hot water it may shrink and felt up. So read care labels, consider the results, and whenever you are unsure, test first!

PLANT FIBERS Also called cellulose fibers, these are basically any fibers that come from a plant; fabrics include cotton, linen, rayon, hemp, and Tencel. Fiber-reactive dyes are calibrated for these fabrics, so you can assume that most of them will yield results similar to what's shown on the bottle, with cotton producing the truest, or most accurate, colors. Most of these fabrics are easily washable so they are great to use for everyday clothing, home decor, and children's items. The color comes out especially vivid on cotton, so it is a great fabric choice when you want bright, true colors.

ANIMAL FIBERS Also referred to as protein fibers, these are fibers derived from animals, such as wool and silk. Although fiber-reactive dyes are not made for use on protein fibers, they can still yield wonderful results. However, the outcome is less predictable, especially on deeper and more neutral colors, so if you want to be certain of the color, always test a swatch before starting your project. And if you can't get the results you want with these dyes (for

example, you won't be able to dye silk a true black), try another type of dye instead, such as acid dyes (see page 153). Silk is a personal favorite for dyeing—the smooth, rich texture allows for subtle watercolor effects; deep, rich colors; and stunning detail in your design. Ordinary dye techniques can yield extraordinary results, and can therefore be a great way to create a unique piece for a special occasion.

SYNTHETICS AND BLENDS Fiber-reactive dyes won't bond with polyester, nylon, acrylic, spandex, or any other synthetic fiber. Blends made up of two or more types of fibers may hold some of the dye, basically in proportion to the amount of natural fibers in the fabric. So while a 95 percent cotton, 5 percent spandex jersey fabric will take the dye quite well, a 50–50 blend is less likely to dye well or evenly. This holds true for thread as well, and because many manufactured clothes are sewn with polyester thread for strength, the thread may remain the original color when you dye your clothes. PFD (prepared for dying) clothes are often sewn with cotton thread (see page 156 for where to shop), and if you are sewing your own clothes, you can also use cotton thread to avoid this.

(Below) I dyed both of these shirts in the same color palette. The colors come out true, or accurate, on the cotton T-shirt (right), but notice how they shift on the silk blouse (left). Some colors shift dramatically; the black appears as fuchsia, and the brown as a deep red.

FABRICS PREPARED FOR DYEING You can dye any natural fabric with fiber-reactive dyes, but there are also a few specific types of fabrics and finished garments specifically made for dyeing.

MERCERIZED COTTON has been treated to make it stronger, more lustrous, and easier to dye.

GREIGE GOODS are typically unbleached, undyed, and untreated fabrics or garments. These are sometimes cheaper and are often ready to be dyed.

PFD (PREPARED FOR DYEING) refers to fabrics or garments that have been made specifically to be dyed. They have usually been cleaned and bleached without the use of optical whiteners, which can react poorly with dyes. PFD garments are also often made with dyeable thread and cut larger to account for shrinkage.

TIP *Fabric (especially rayon) is more fragile when wet, so be careful while tying and untying, washing, and wringing out your garments.*

TESTING, TESTING

WASH TEST A good rule of thumb is if fabric can be washed, it can be dyed. Despite the "dry clean only" labels on many silk garments, you will find that as long as they are washed carefully, without much agitation and taking care not to "shock" the fibers by moving quickly from hot to cold or vice versa, these fabrics may not actually require dry cleaning. Wool may be more trouble. If you're not sure whether your fabric is washable, do a wash test on a small piece before dyeing the entire thing. Before testing your fabric, cut a duplicate piece of fabric or trace it onto a piece of paper so you can compare them for texture changes and shrinkage after washing.

BURN TEST If you're unsure what your fabric is made of, do a burn test. Pay attention to the way the fabric ignites, the smoke and smell it produces as it burns, and the residue that it leaves behind. Natural fibers will burn and turn to soft ashes; and animal fibers will produce a burnt-hair smell. Synthetics tend to burn with a dark smoke and strong smell, and then melt and bead up. Blends may be harder to distinguish. Please perform all burn tests with caution.

REDUCE, REUSE, RECYCLE

Tie-dye is inherently environmentally friendly; it has been used for centuries to give new life to old clothing and reduce the need for new production and landfill waste. By choosing wisely and acting thoughtfully, you can further minimize your personal impact on the environment while enjoying your new hobby.

REDUCE The one thing you can't do without in tie-dye is water, so I am always very aware of minimizing my water use whenever possible. Instead of allowing water to run needlessly down the drain, I fill buckets of cool water as soon as I turn on the faucet, waiting for hot water to heat up. If I dye a small project, I wash it out quickly by hand, but with multiple projects it is often more efficient to wash them together in a machine (make sure you are washing out similar colors and not overloading the machine). Last, I try to mix only the amounts of dye and soda ash that I know I'm going to use, unless I'm planning on keeping them around for continual use.

REUSE If I made too much soda ash or bottled dye, I keep the leftovers and reuse them until they are all gone, rather than discard and remix them each time. Although bath dyes quickly lose their strength and can't be used a second time for the same color results, you can throw in old T-shirts, dish towels, or quilting fabric right after removing your project and see what wonderful surprise you come up with!

Most of your tools can be reused as well. Even your rubber bands, plastic bags, rubber gloves, and tarps can be rinsed and used again and again.

RECYCLE The best tools are often things I would have thrown out: plastic yogurt and take-out containers, old kitchen equipment, or new-to-you items from thrift stores. The plastic utensil packet that comes with your take-out dinner works as a great on-the-go tie-dye kit; there's a spoon for measuring your dye, a knife for leveling it, a fork for mixing, and a white napkin for testing your color results!

I always keep a stack of old rags, tired dish towels, and stained T-shirts lying around to clean up messes and dry off my tools and hands while I'm working. This way I rarely have to use paper towels. You can also use rags instead of newspaper to soak up excess dye.

Here is an example of the same gray dye on a variety of fabrics. Notice how it appears pink on protein fibers such as silk and wool, compared to the more accurate gray on cellulose fibers. You can also see the different patterns that may result depending on the texture of the fabric.

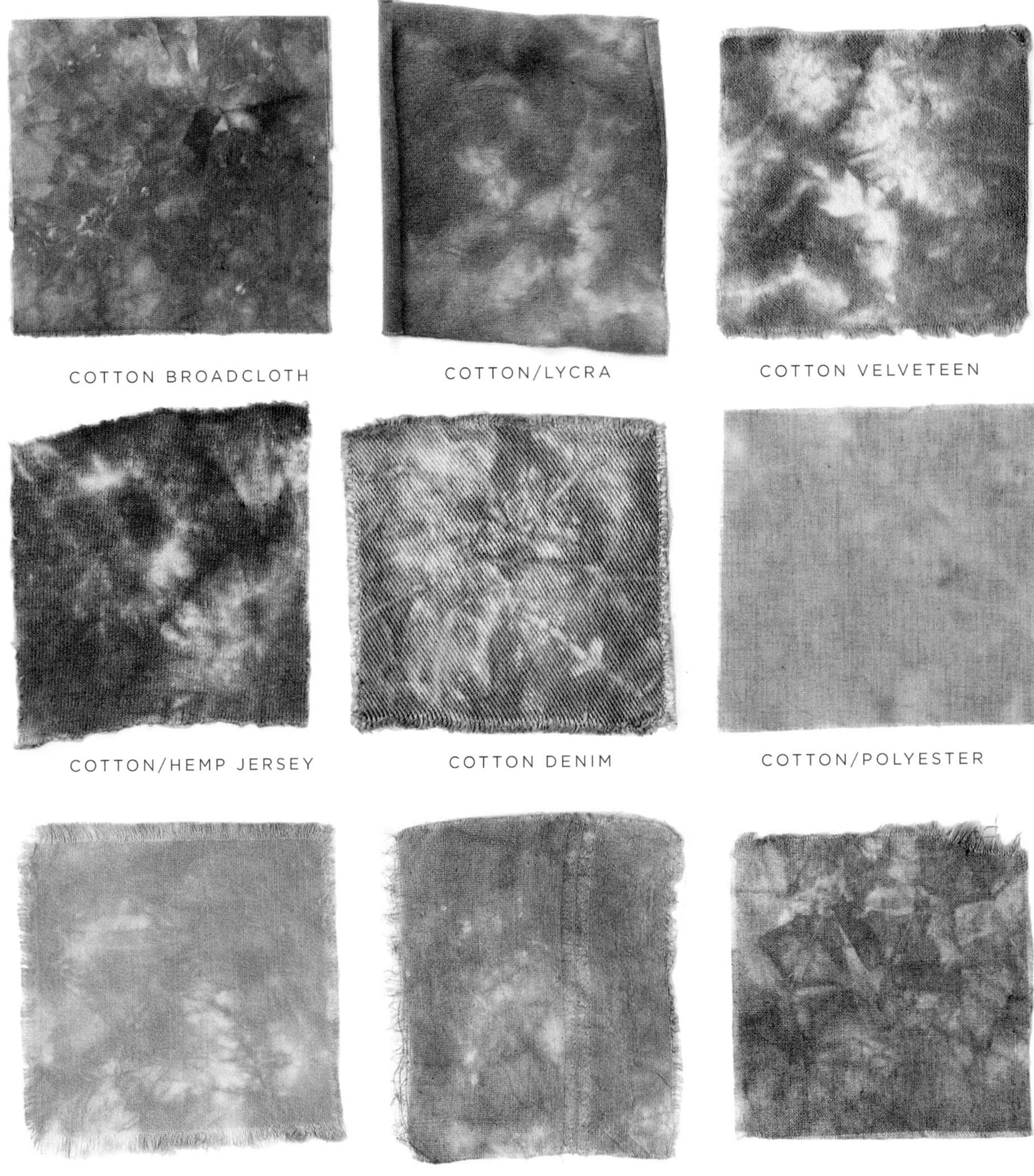

COTTON BROADCLOTH

COTTON/LYCRA

COTTON VELVETEEN

COTTON/HEMP JERSEY

COTTON DENIM

COTTON/POLYESTER

BAMBOO RAYON DOBBY

PINEAPPLE FIBER

LINEN

SILK CHARMEUSE

SILK HABOTAI

SILK CHIFFON

RAW SILK

SILK GAUZE

SILK CREPE DE CHINE

SILK/WOOL

SILK/HEMP

SILK/RAYON VELVET

DESIGN CHOICES

Tie-dye is all about playing around with colors and patterns; it's wonderfully versatile and fun to work with. And after many experiments, I've discovered that it can be used to make a subtle and refined piece, an extremely splashy statement, or anything in between. As with any other medium—painting, printing, sewing, or knitting—once you learn the basic techniques, the options are endless. Think about the fabrics you are working with and the colors you choose. Keep in mind basic design principles such as negative and positive space, size, repetition, and balance. Picture where you are going to wear this garment, and what mood you want it to convey. Are you trying to create an eye-popping statement or a sophisticated and understated look? Begin to develop an understanding of the aesthetic you are going for, and use these elements to help create it.

EASY COLOR THEORY

If you ever took an art class, you might remember the basics: primary colors, warm and cool colors, and neutrals. In hand dyeing, because of the way colors interact, there are additional concepts to consider that make it even more fun, like the way colors blend on fabric or the fact that time plays an active role in the final design. Don't worry if art was never your thing; knowing about color may help you plan your projects, but half the fun of tie-dye is the unexpected, and you can really never go wrong!

THE PRIMARIES There are two main sets of color primaries. Additive colors are based on the primary colors of light (red, green, and blue) and when combined create white. This RGB method is used with televisions, computer screens, and projectors. Subtractive colors are based on the primary colors of pigments and dyes (cyan, magenta, and yellow) and when combined create black. This CMYK method is the one we use for dyeing; it is also used for printing color photographs and with all paints and inks. The basic primaries (red, blue, and yellow) that you learned in kindergarten were developed before scientific color theorists established the RGB and CMYK methods, and are in fact outdated and rarely used by professionals or artists anymore.

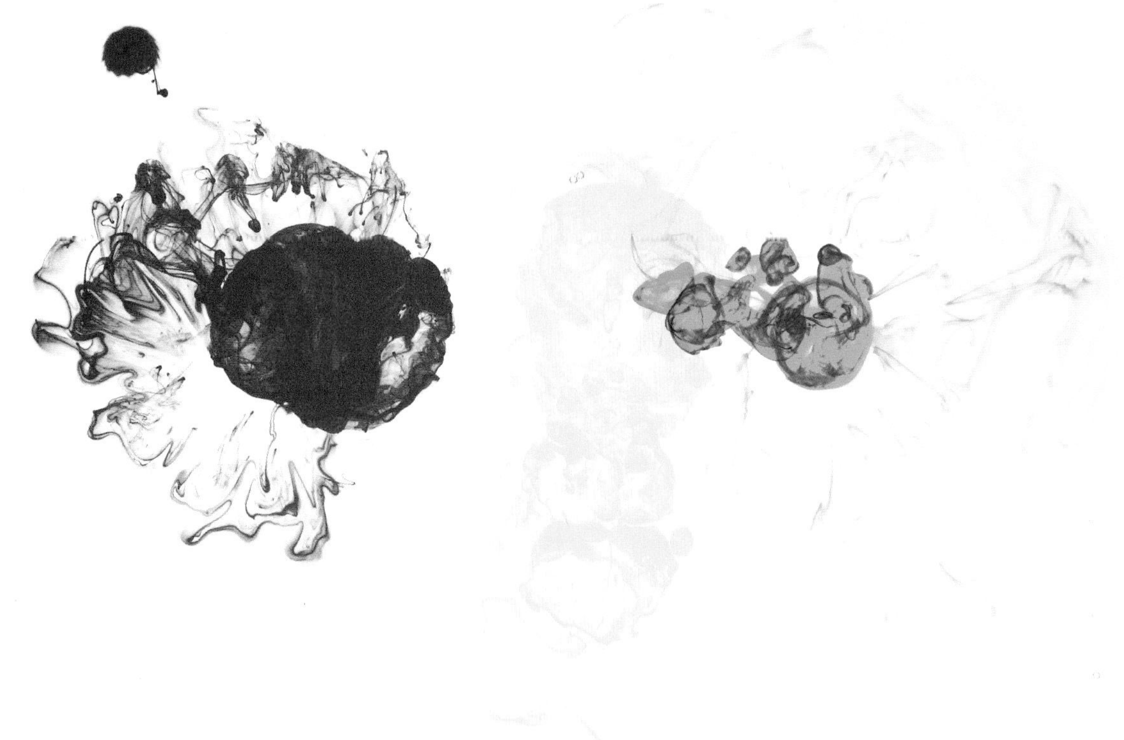

HUE Hue refers to the basic color as it appears on the color wheel. In tie-dye, the primary colors are turquoise, fuchsia, and yellow. You can mix two of these primary colors together to create the secondary colors—blue, red, and green—and further mix to create tertiary colors and all other possible hues. A comprehensive color wheel would include countless hues, exponential mixtures of the primaries. With that in mind, feel free to branch off from the expected colors and work with ones that suit you. This color wheel represents the basic colors, but adjusted to my taste. I've pulled colors for the projects in the book from this wheel.

VALUE Value refers to how light or dark a color is. By mixing a pure color with black, we create shades of that color. Usually, by mixing a pure color with white you create tints, but because there is no white dye, we do this by using water instead. A higher proportion of water is necessary to make the same impact that black makes on the original color, and black will alter a color very quickly, so add it slowly until you achieve the color you want.

SATURATION Saturation refers to a color's intensity. By mixing a color with its complement (the color opposite in the color wheel), you can tone down the intensity and create a subtler or earthier version of that color. Gray can also be used to create tones. In tie-dye, you can alter the saturation of a color by mixing dyes together before applying them to the garment, or by applying complements close to each other so they bleed and overlap. Make sure you don't accidentally do this if you want bright, pure colors!

PLAYING WITH TIME

Time also plays an active role in tie-dyeing; this is part of what makes it so magical. How long you dye a piece of fabric will affect the final results. The amount of time that has passed since mixing your dyes will alter the color. Leaving a project sitting longer will allow more time for different colors to run and blend.

Most colors will become darker over a longer curing time, but they may develop other effects as well, such as stronger colorfastness or changes in hue. This occurs because most dye colors are a mix of different base dyes that each have their own reaction time, so while curing, the color may shift warmer or cooler.

Value: Create shades by adding black

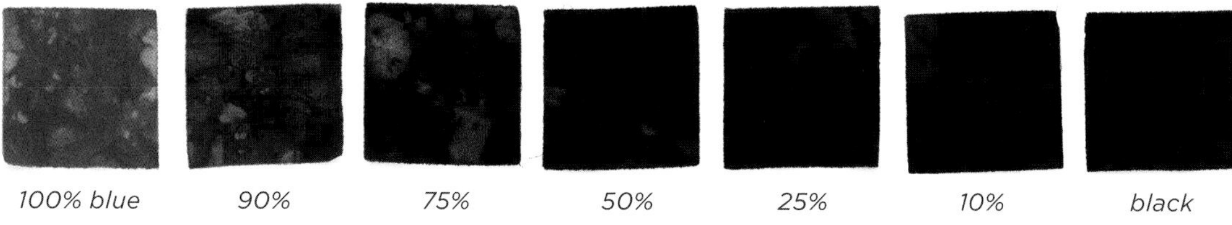

100% blue | *90%* | *75%* | *50%* | *25%* | *10%* | *black*

Value: Create tints by adding water

100% blue | *90%* | *75%* | *50%* | *25%* | *10%* | *water*

Saturation: Create tones by adding a complement color

100% blue | *90%* | *75%* | *50%* | *25%* | *10%* | *complement*

Saturation: Create tones by adding gray

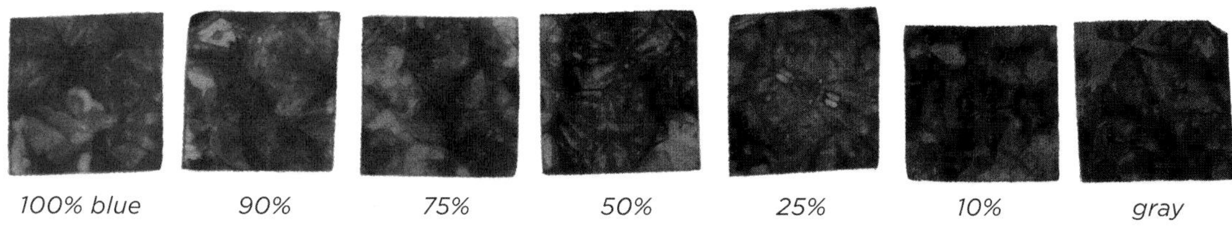

100% blue | *90%* | *75%* | *50%* | *25%* | *10%* | *gray*

Time: Length of curing time will alter the hue and value of a color

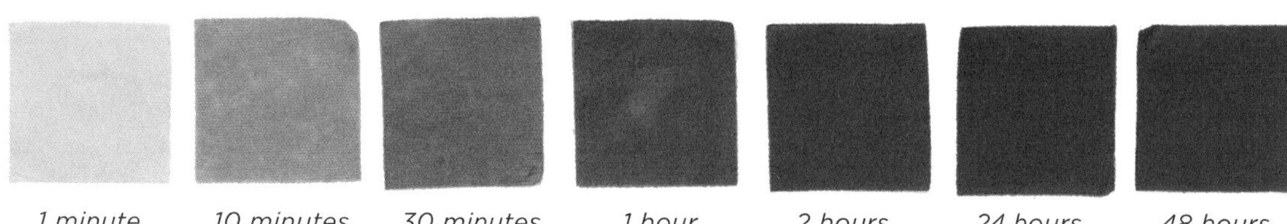

1 minute | *10 minutes* | *30 minutes* | *1 hour* | *2 hours* | *24 hours* | *48 hours*

COLOR MIXING

Dye is applied as a liquid and tends to bleed, so colors placed next to each other will often overlap and mix. In addition to the basic color theory concepts, it is important to think about how colors will react when combined in a bottle or used together on one dye project. When used on the same project, a yellow dye and a blue dye are likely to blend and give you green. Complementary colors placed next to each other may blend and create a muddy brown, so choose carefully when using a lot of colors together in one dye project. Use this chart to help you mix your own dye colors, and also to choose which colors will work well when placed next to each other.

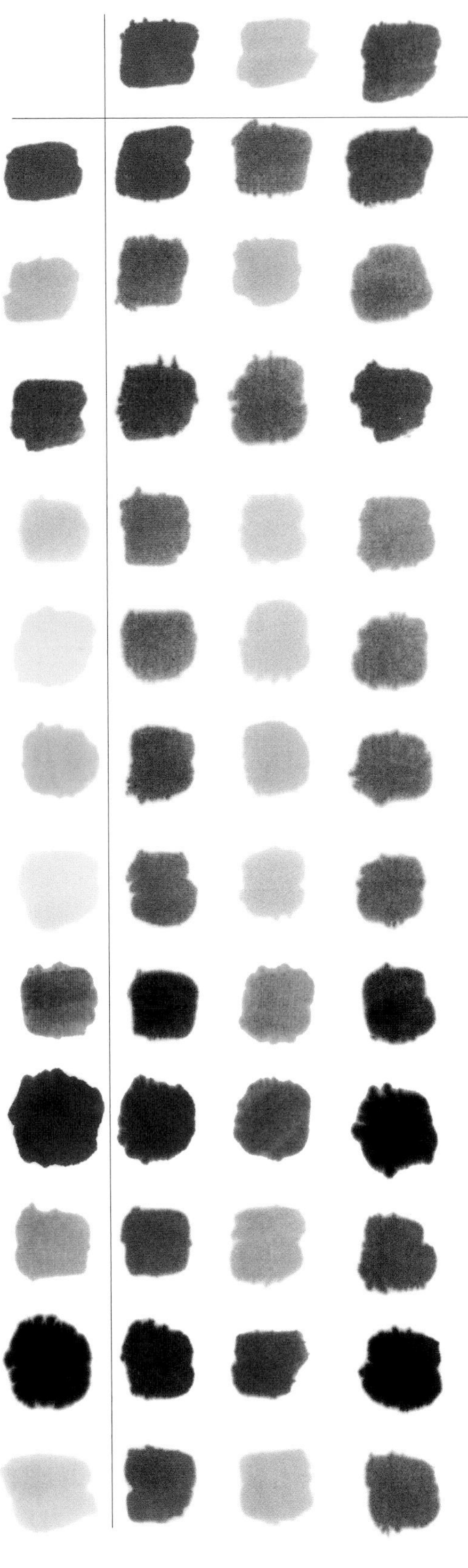

THE COMPLEXITY OF A SINGLE COLOR

All dye colors are made from the same few base dyes. Each dye reacts differently with the fabric and the water; fuchsia tends to be more difficult to mix up completely, for example, while turquoise takes longer to wash out. Certain colors come out as expected on silk, while others create wildly unpredictable results. Therefore, whether you are mixing your own color or buying a premade dye, you may find that the basic elements react differently on your fabric. One color may spread farther than the others, forming a halo, or creating a subtle multicolored effect. Some dyes may take longer to fully cure. The same factors create the unexpected results in an "exhausted" dye bath, because one base dye may still be active while another is completely spent.

(Below) Gray dye powder as it dissolves in water. Notice how it is made up of multiple base dyes that when blended will create a neutral gray.

CHOOSING COLORS

Your color palette can be your most powerful design element, and can make all the difference between so-so and spectacular garments. Colors can set a mood, make a statement, and create a feeling of warmth or tranquility, elegance or playfulness. The color schemes that follow are basic suggestions to help you choose your color palettes. Keep in mind the fluid nature of tie-dye; while you may choose only two colors from the color wheel, they are likely to blend together and create additional colors.

WARM — COOL — ANALOGOUS

COMPLEMENTARY — TRIADIC — TETRADIC

SPLIT COMPLEMENTS — NEUTRALS — MONOCHROMATIC

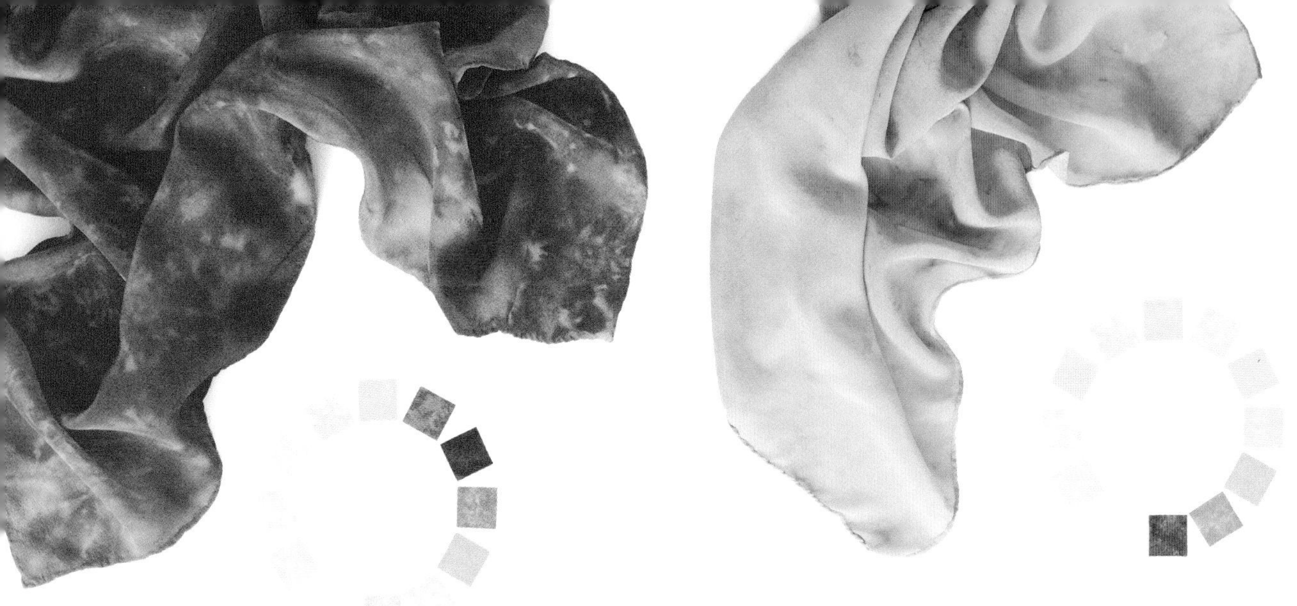

WARM colors, generally reds, oranges, and yellows, are energizing and comforting. They tend to be easy to work with because the colors blend seamlessly with expected results.

COOL colors, generally blues, greens, and purples, tend to be calming and soothing. Beyond this, you can actually find a warm or cool version of any color, such as a tomato red (warm) or raspberry red (cool).

ANALOGOUS colors are those next to each other on the color wheel. They are often harmonious and easy to use in tie-dye, since overlapping colors will blend well and you won't get any muddy browns.

COMPLEMENTARY colors are directly across from each other on the color wheel. The contrast can be both vibrant and intense, and should be used carefully, because complements placed closely will mix and become muddied or brown.

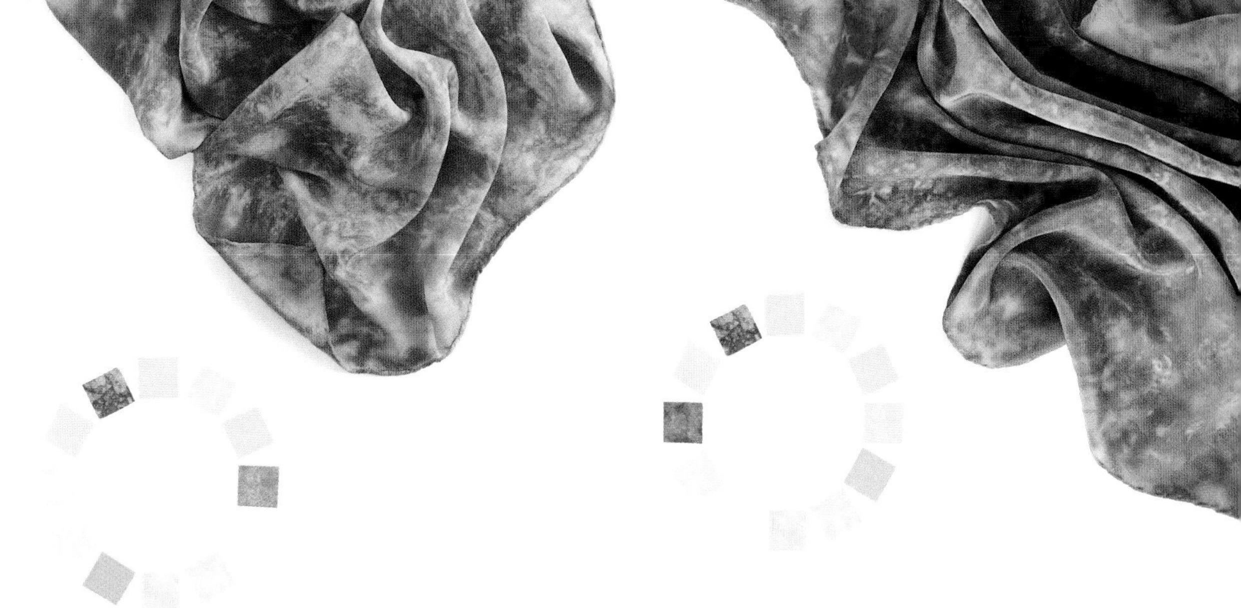

TRIADIC color schemes can be made by choosing three colors evenly spaced on the color wheel. They are bright and vibrant like the complementary color scheme but provide more balance.

TETRADIC color schemes can be made by pairing two complementary color pairs. They work best when one color is allowed to dominate, and the rest are used as supplementary and accent colors.

SPLIT COMPLEMENTS include a main color and the two colors adjacent to its complement. They have the strong contrast of the complementary colors without as much tension.

NEUTRALS are colors that are so toned down they appear to have no strong hue. Black and white are true neutrals; grays, browns, and tans are also neutral but lean to either the warm or cool side. Neutrals tend to go well with most colors.

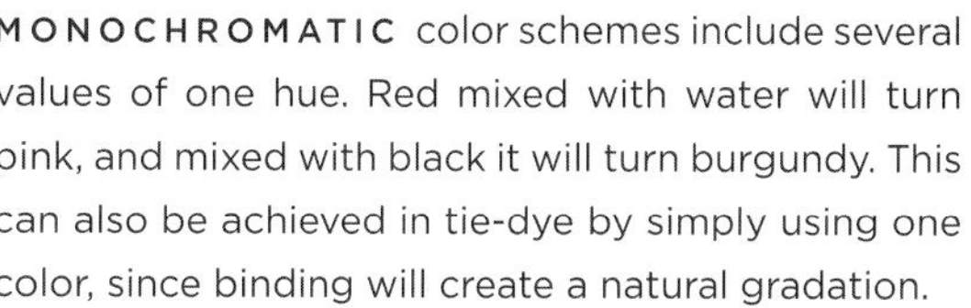

MONOCHROMATIC color schemes include several values of one hue. Red mixed with water will turn pink, and mixed with black it will turn burgundy. This can also be achieved in tie-dye by simply using one color, since binding will create a natural gradation.

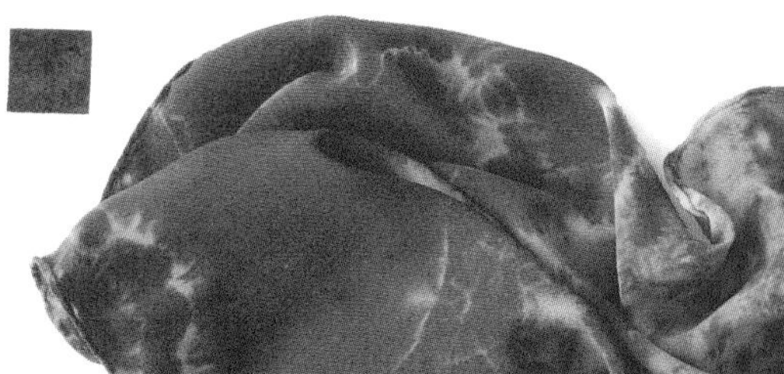

ADVANCED THINKING

There's still more! Now that you understand the basics of fabrics, colors, and dye mixtures, you can begin to use these principles along with additional elements of design to create interesting pieces. Surprisingly varied results can be obtained by playing with color ratios or composition, or by experimenting with additional design concepts specific to hand dyeing based on the dye's transparent nature.

OVERDYEING You don't have to feel trapped working with only a basic white background. Once you feel comfortable understanding how different colors react together, you can play around with overdyeing colored fabric. Consider how the color of your fabric will interact with the dyes you are choosing, and try the same dye on different backgrounds.

(Above) These T-shirts were created using the knotting technique (page 117).

BLEACHING Using either chlorine bleach or a specially formulated discharge paste, you can use the same tie-dye processes to remove the color from your fabric. Bleaching will basically give you the reverse effect of dyeing, but you want to be careful as bleach can be more unpleasant to work with than dye. Bleach will also continue to operate even after washing, so use a bleach stopping aid (available where you buy your dye) to make your design permanent and keep the bleach from eating away at your fabric. All fabrics will not discharge equally; some may bleach to white, while others may reveal an array of pale hues.

(Above) These T-shirts were made using the spiral technique (page 97),

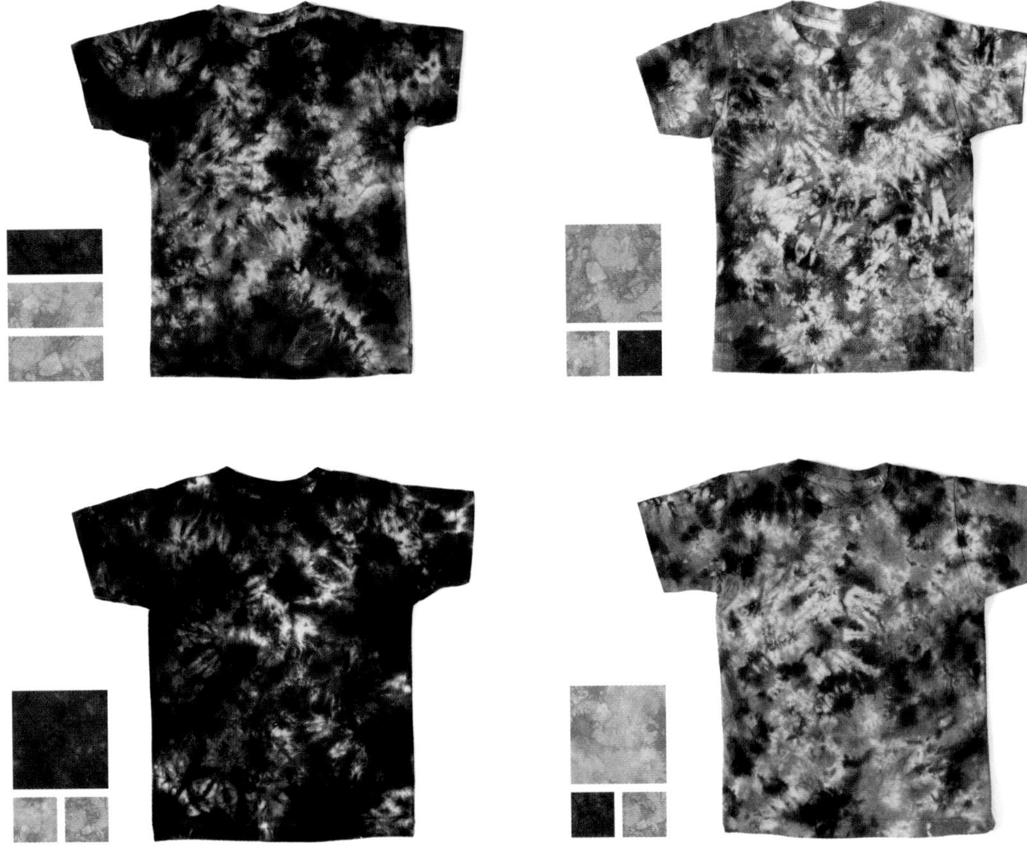

COLOR RATIOS The same colors added in different ratios will create very different effects. A 1:1 ratio will create tension, while giving one color dominance will create a more balanced harmony. You can change the look dramatically depending on which color you allow to dominate. In many of my tie-dye projects I choose one or two colors to act as my main colors, and use others as accents. You don't need to be precise about this; just use more of one color and less of the other.

(Above) These T-shirts were made using the scrunch technique (page 81).

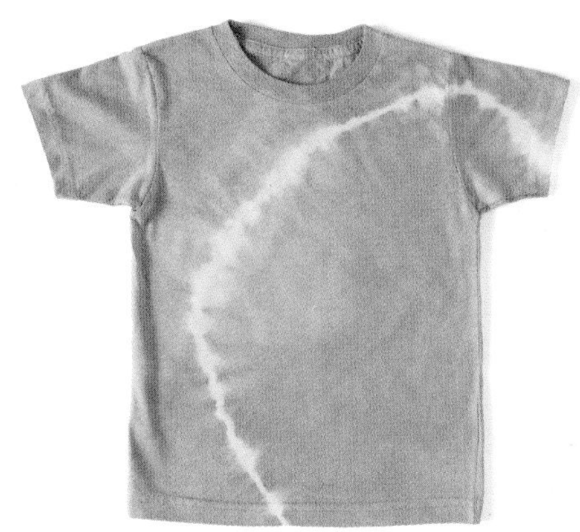

COMPOSITION The final design tool you have at your disposal may be just as important as color choice. Creating your composition can set a tone and help draw the eye. While much of tie-dye is up to chance, and with many techniques you will not choose where every scrunch or wrinkle is placed, you still have plenty of room for making design decisions. Consider variety, size, repetition, placement, and balance when designing your piece. Center a design on the chest or off to the side. Shrink it down or enlarge it so that it goes off the edges of the garment. Use a single element, repeat a motif, or create a continuous design that covers the entire garment seamlessly. Mix and match different tying methods and use them together. Try tying only part of the garment, and keep the rest undyed or dye it a solid color. The possibilities are endless!

(Above) These T-shirts were made using the circle technique (page 89).

TIP *When centering a design on your garment, the center of your design should actually be more in line with the armpits than the true center of the shirt. This way the design will draw the eye up toward the face and away from the belly.*

HOW TO TIE-DYE

There are two basic tie-dye methods: direct application and immersion. Direct application methods include bottle dyeing and hand painting; they allow for versatility, control, and the ability to use many colors together in one project. This is how exuberant and colorful tie-dye is made. Immersion dyeing creates a more uniform coloring, is generally used for monochromatic effects, and is often more refined and elegant. The same dyes are used for both methods, but depending on which you choose, the dyes are mixed in different ways and at different strengths. As long as fabric, dye, and soda ash are involved, you can work in any order and still get wonderful and permanent results.

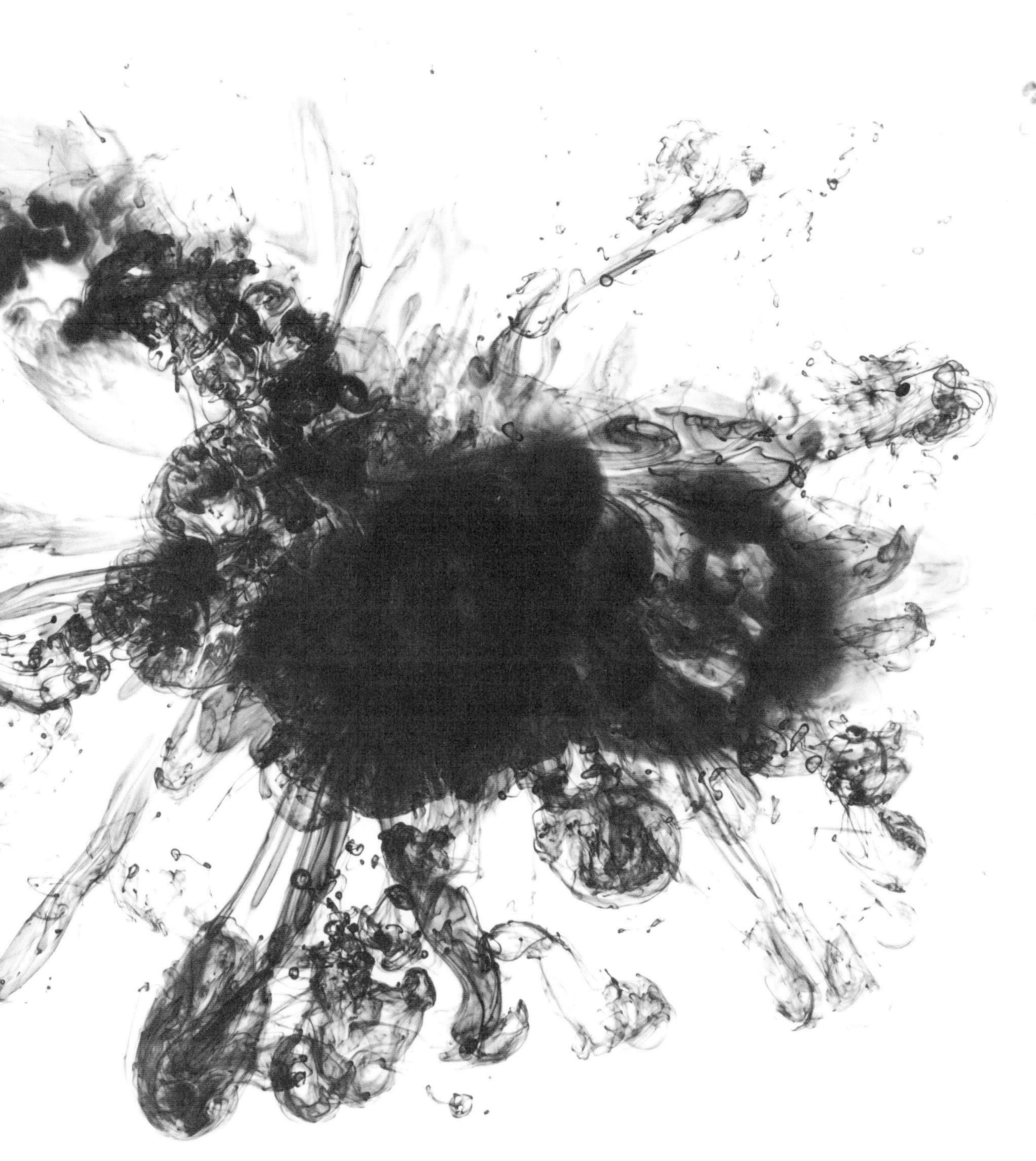

DIRECT APPLICATION DYEING

Direct application, often applied with a plastic squeeze bottle, is how the tie-dye most of us are familiar with is created. Using the bottle allows for a great level of control over the design since each color is applied individually, so it is the best method for achieving bright, multicolored dye effects.

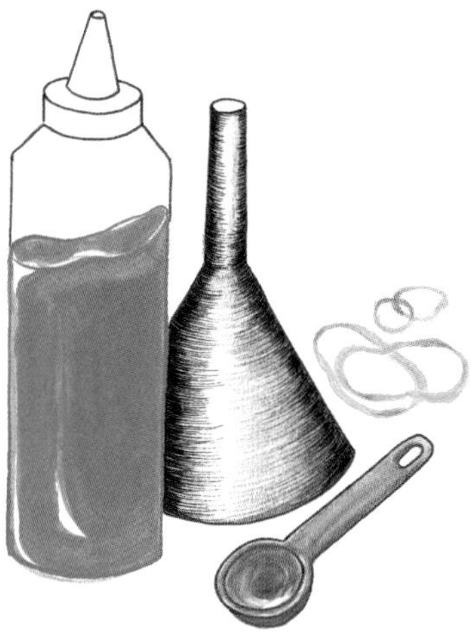

STEP 1. PREPARING THE FABRIC
Wash your fabric before dyeing to remove fabric sizing (the chemicals left on the fabric from manufacturing) and any grease or dirt that may be on the fabric. This will ensure even coverage of dye.

TIP *Of course, since you're tie-dyeing, you may not care if your colors are even, so wash or don't wash—it's your call. While it's not always necessary, you will find that certain fabrics do benefit from it, like canvas, anything feeling obviously starchy, or old clothes that might need a good cleaning.*

STEP 2. SETTING UP
Read through the project materials list and set up your space as described on page 20 so everything is ready for use. Once you begin the process it's hard to stop and get things you forgot (at least without leaving a trail of dye through your house!).

HAPPY ACCIDENTS *These hand towels were created as a by-product of my regular tie-dye process. When I was setting up, instead of laying newspaper on the table to catch the excess dye, I used towels, and the spilled dye created exciting patterns. Try doing this with other things, like a tote bag or T-shirt, and see what happy accidents you create!*

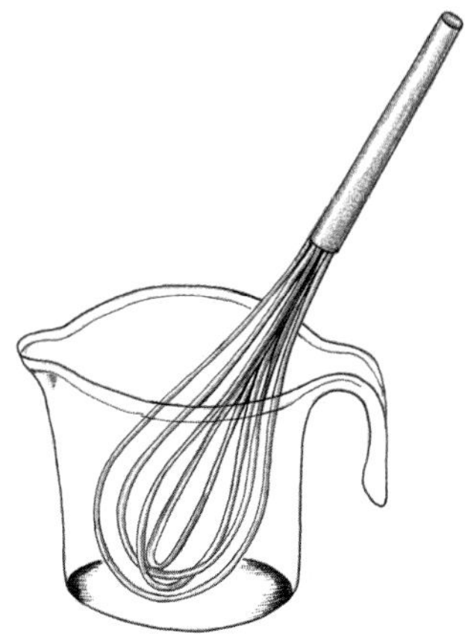

STEP 3. SODA ASH PRESOAK

For bright true colors, add 1 cup (250 ml) of soda ash to 1 gallon (4 l) of water. Although the soda ash doesn't require heat to be activated, you will find it is easier to melt the powder in warm water. Always add the soda ash to the water to avoid clumping, not the other way around, and stir vigorously as you add it. Soak the fabric in the soda ash for 30 minutes. As little as 5 minutes will work, but this will yield subtler colors. If you are using a delicate fabric like silk, a shorter presoak might be a good idea. Wring out the excess liquid so the fabric is damp, but not dripping.

TIP *A gallon will soak around ten T-shirts, and you can multiply the recipe for as much presoak solution as you need. It's okay if the garments are crammed tightly together; just make sure that all of the fabric is fully saturated.*

ALTERNATIVE *If you're tie-dyeing with kids, you might want to use a milder chemical bath to protect their skin from splashes (or if their gloves come off). Use less soda ash with the same amount of water; just know that the results will be a little more muted.*

STEP 4. (OPTIONAL) PREPARING THE CHEMICAL WATER

I usually like to keep things simple and don't often use additives, but they can be especially helpful with certain dye projects like painting and ombré, or when trying to achieve the elusive true black. I do use them in a few of the projects in this book.

If you decide to use additives, mix them up first to create a chemical solution. Make one large batch and use it to mix the individual dye colors. You can store the chemical solution in a closed container in the refrigerator for a few weeks so you don't have to remix it each time. Just be sure to label it well and keep it away from the food in your fridge.

Working with these proportions, adapt the recipe to create the total amount of chemical water you will need. If you don't want to use these additives, you can skip this step and use regular tap water instead.

OPTIONAL ADDITIVES

CHEMICAL	HOW TO MIX	WHAT IT DOES	WHEN TO USE
UREA	Dissolve 1 tablespoon urea in 1 cup (250 ml) warm water and let cool before adding the dye.	Helps dissolve the dye and avoid explosions of undissolved dye powder; also keeps the fabric wet longer during the curing process.	Avoiding dye explosions can be helpful in all dye methods, and the wetting aspect can be especially useful when you are leaving projects out for a long curing period.
CALSOLENE OIL	Add ½ teaspoon per gallon (4 l) of water.	Helps break the surface tension and increase the evenness of dyeing.	Useful for immersion dye methods, in particular when trying to achieve an ombré effect. It can also be used to help dissolve the dye more easily.
SODIUM ALGINATE	Sprinkle in ⅛ to 1 teaspoon per cup of water and mix well. Don't add too much; it will take about an hour to thicken to its full effect. Sodium alginate is made from seaweed, so refrigerate the leftovers.	Thickens the dye to decrease bleeding and allow more control over designs.	Useful if you want more precision in your tie-dyeing. Also good for direct application methods like painting on fabric.

STEP 5. MIXING THE DYES

Mix the dyes using either your chemical water or room-temperature tap water. Spoon the powder into the bottle through a dry funnel, add a small amount of water, replace the lid, and shake vigorously. Fill the bottle with the remainder of the water and shake again.

Mixing calculations will vary based on the color, its chemical makeup, and the manufacturer, so read the instructions that come with your dye. Also, when using darker colors it may be necessary to increase the amount of dye powder. Feel free to mix and match your own colors and tints, or make pastels by using less dye powder. Precise measurements aren't always necessary with so many unpredictable variables (see page 65); however, I like to keep track of my measurements in case I want to try to replicate results in the future. You can use this chart as a general guide.

TIP *Make sure to replace the lid on the dye powder immediately after using it so that you don't accidentally get water inside it or spill powder all over your work space.*

MIXING CALCULATIONS
FOR DIRECT APPLICATION

ADULT T-SHIRTS	TOTAL H_2O	DYE POWDER
1	½ CUP (125 ML)	1 TSP
2	1 CUP (250 ML)	2 TSP
4	2 CUPS (500 ML)	4 TSP
8	1 QUART (1 L)	8 TSP

ALTERNATIVE: ALL-IN-ONE METHOD

Rather than presoaking, you can mix the soda ash directly in the dye bottle; just add 1 teaspoon of soda ash per 1 cup (250 ml) of water. Although not usually preferable, this method can be a useful alternative if you are working with dry garments (as in the Classic Striped Tee on page 118 and the Lattice Tablecloth on page 122); or when you are dyeing with a large group of people and don't want the mess or time of the soda ash soak. Remember that after an hour the dyes will begin to lose strength, and after 24 hours they will be completely inactive, so you won't be able to keep these dyes for later use.

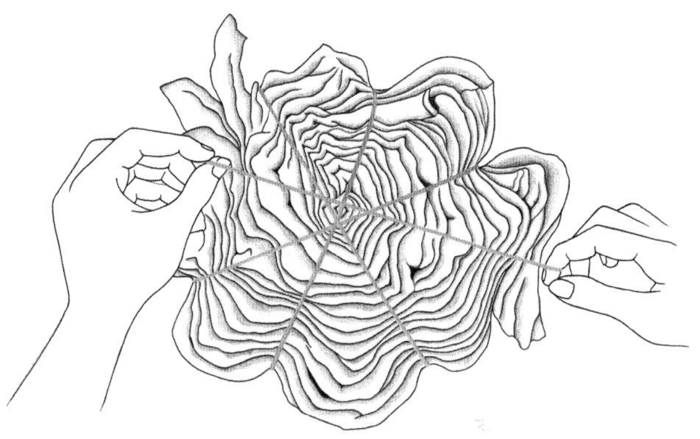

STEP 6. TYING

You can tie, fold, or bind your garment in various designs either before soaking them or after. Damp fabric is often easier to manipulate, while dry fabric allows the ease of working at a leisurely pace (I've spent many hours watching movies on my couch while tying large dye projects).

The projects in this book use a variety of different methods, including scrunching, circles, spirals, stripes, folding and stitching, as well as a few untied techniques. These techniques can be used individually or in combination. In general, you want to tie fabric looser and flatter when dyeing with direct application than when immersion dyeing, to allow for more control over where you apply your dyes.

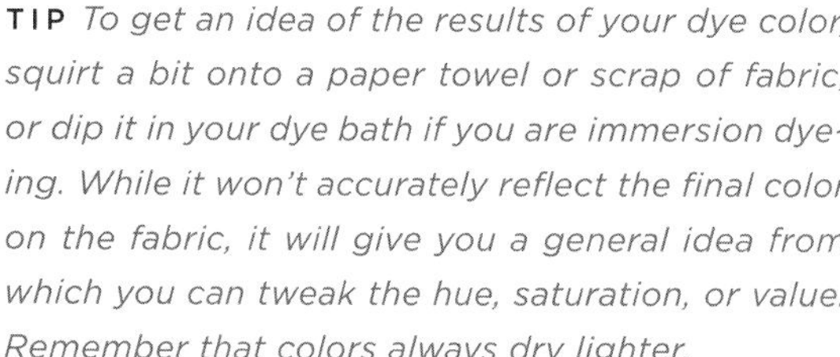

TIP *To get an idea of the results of your dye color, squirt a bit onto a paper towel or scrap of fabric, or dip it in your dye bath if you are immersion dyeing. While it won't accurately reflect the final color on the fabric, it will give you a general idea from which you can tweak the hue, saturation, or value. Remember that colors always dry lighter.*

TIP *Lay your fabric on a clean, covered work surface to tie. Plastic is best because it allows you to move wet fabric around easily. Save the newspaper for when it's time to dye because it absorbs moisture and makes tying difficult.*

Make sure to wipe down your work surface before placing your garment on it; even one minuscule speck of dye powder can create a big color burst on wet fabric!

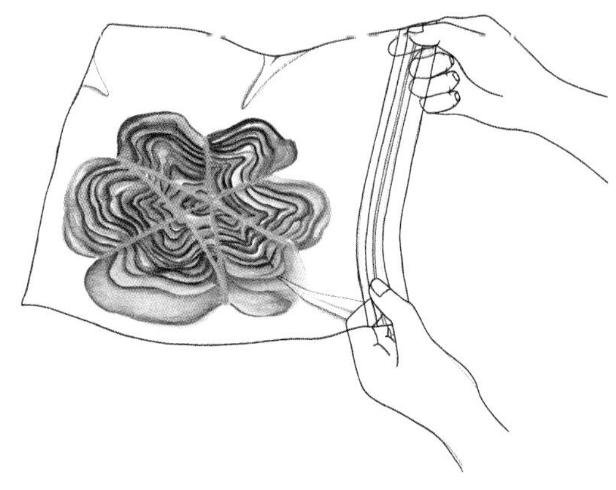

STEP 7. DYEING

Now you're ready to dye! Pick out your colors, keeping in mind the possible mixtures that overlapping colors will create (see page 40). There are many methods for applying dye, but a tried-and-true tie-dye favorite is to apply it directly to the fabric using squeeze bottles.

Place the garment on some newspaper or on a grate over a shallow container to catch excess dye. Apply the dye liberally, making sure to get the bottle's nozzle deep inside the folds. There will always be more undyed fabric than you can see, so saturate well if you don't want too much left undyed.

After you dye the first side, flip your fabric over to dye the second side. If you have been applying the dye liberally, a lot of the color will have soaked through, and you won't need to add as much to the second side.

How you apply the dye can change the outcome as much as how you tie it. With the same tying technique, you can get vastly different results depending on whether you use the dye liberally or sparingly, use one color or many, or apply the colors in a regimented way or randomly (see the Spiral Tees on page 97).

STEP 8. CURING

Okay, this is the hard part. You're going to have to sit back and wait for the results! For direct application methods such as bottle tie-dyeing or painting, you need to keep the fabric wet and chemically active during the entire curing process. Put it inside a plastic bag or cover it with a tarp—whatever keeps it from drying out. You can leave it to cure from 6 hours to 2 days, but the general rule of thumb to achieve bright true colors is 6 hours for silk and 24 hours for cotton and other fabrics. A longer curing time is helpful when it is cold out. After 2 days the chemicals will have lost all of their active power.

STEP 9. THE REVEAL

My favorite part! Rinse the finished garment under cold running water until the water runs clear. Raise the water temperature and continue to rinse under warm water as you remove the rubber bands and reveal the results. Once the water is running clear again you can either throw the item directly into the washing machine or wash it by hand (either way, wash it separately the first time you wash it in the machine). If you have dyed more than one project, wash only like colors together in the machine. Launder according to the care label on your garment, on as hot a setting as it allows. Use Synthrapol, made especially for use in dyeing, or a mild dish or laundry detergent to wash out the excess dye and keep the colors from getting muddy during the wash. You can also help avoid muddy results by not overloading your machine. After the initial wash or two, the excess dye should all be removed and your garment can be laundered regularly.

TIP *You will be amazed at what a quick pass of a hot iron can do. Iron your garments after you finish and the subtleties of your design will spring to life!*

STEP 10. CLEANUP

STORAGE The soda ash solution itself can be kept and reused until it's all gone. The dyes will stay good for about a week, and if you aren't concerned with getting consistent results, they can be labeled and stored in a cool dark space for a few weeks. They cannot be kept if you mix soda ash in the same container with them.

DISPOSAL Because the dyes and soda ash are relatively nontoxic, you can dispose of them as you would any household cleanser or detergent. It's better to pour them down the drain than into your garden, as undiluted dyes and soda ash can raise the pH and sodium levels in soil and create a hostile growing environment.

CLEANING Clean soda ash out of containers and tools to ensure it doesn't affect later dye processes. You can tell if it is still there because it has a slightly slimy feel, and it leaves a white residue after it dries. Rinse your sink or tub right away if you've used it to wash your supplies and projects. And always wash your hands after dyeing and before cooking or eating.

IMMERSION DYEING

This method is generally used for solid dyeing or monochromatic effects such as traditional Japanese indigo-dyed *shibori*. These are the instructions for the standard method of immersion dyeing, but there are many variations, a few of which I will also introduce. Immersion dyeing is great for graphic, monochromatic patterns, and subtle effects, or simply when you're short on time and want to see the results quickly, since it doesn't require a long curing process.

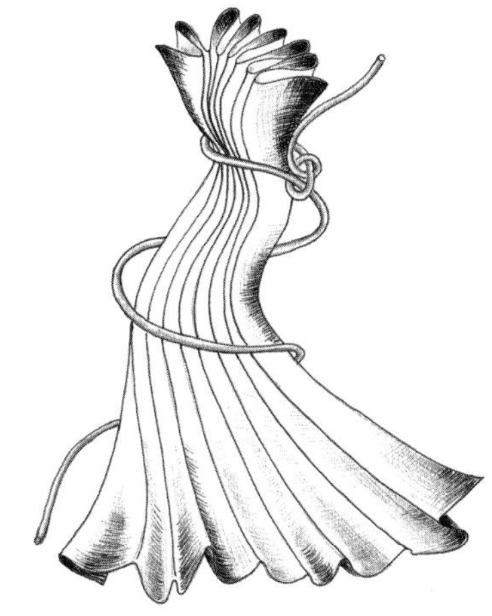

STEP 1. PREPARING THE FABRIC

Wash your fabric before dyeing to remove fabric sizing (the chemicals left on the fabric from manufacturing) and any grease or dirt that may be on the fabric. This will ensure even coverage of dye.

TIP *Of course, since you are tie-dyeing, you may not care if your colors are even, so wash or don't wash—it's your call. While it's not always necessary, you will find that certain fabrics do benefit from it, like thick canvas, anything feeling obviously starchy, or old clothes that might need a good cleaning.*

STEP 2. SETTING UP

Read through the project materials list and set up your space as described on page 20 so everything is ready for use. Once you begin the process it's hard to stop and get things you forgot (at least without leaving a trail of dye through your house!).

STEP 3. TYING

You can tie, fold, or bind your fabric in various designs either wet or dry. As I mentioned earlier, damp fabric is often easier to manipulate, while dry fabric allows you to work at a leisurely pace. If your technique doesn't include presoaking in soda ash but you still want to work with wet fabric while you tie, simply run it under the faucet and wring it out until damp. You will find that wet and dry fabric give different results when dyed in a dye bath (see the chart on page 66).

You can use the same tying methods for immersion dyeing that you use for bottle dyeing. In general, when immersion dyeing, you will want to tie the rubber bands, string, or clamps tighter than when you are bottle dyeing, to ensure that the dye can't seep in and color the entire garment.

STEP 4. MIXING THE DYE BATH

Choose a bucket large enough to fit your fabric with room to stir. Using the chart below, figure out your total quantities of water, dye, and additives. If you choose to use optional additives such as urea or calsolene oil, see instructions on page 55.

In a separate container, mix the dye powder with a small amount of room-temperature water, stirring well to create a paste. If you choose to use salt, dissolve it in some hot tap water in another container. Add the dye concentrate (and the salt mixture) to your dye bucket, then, using room-temperature water, fill to the recommended total amount of water required for your mixture and stir well.

Depending on the color you wish to achieve, you can use different quantities of dye. Try mixing a few colors together in one dye bath; while you will still get monochromatic results, you will see a richness and depth that wouldn't otherwise be there. Each brand will provide instructions for its own dyes, but you can use this chart as a general guide.

STEP 5. DYEING

Submerge your fabric in the dye bath, first wetting it in water if you wish. Soak for 10 to 15 minutes, stirring to ensure even coverage.

TIP *If your garment keeps floating to the top, try filling some empty bottles with water and placing them on top to submerge the fabric.*

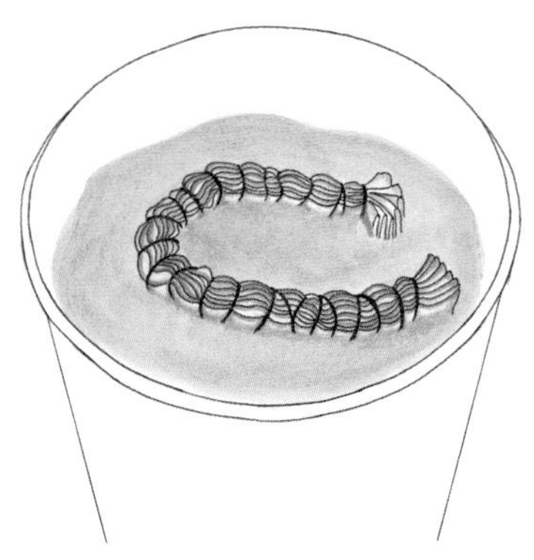

MIXING CALCULATIONS FOR IMMERSION DYEING

FABRIC BY WEIGHT	APPROXIMATE # OF T-SHIRTS	TOTAL H_2O	SODA ASH	NON-IODIZED SALT (optional, or use less)
1 1/2 ounces (38 gms)	Baby Tee	1 qt (1 l)	1 1/2 tsp	1/4 cup (60 ml)
3 ounces (75 gms)	1	2 qts (2 l)	1 tbsp	1/2 cup (125 ml)
6 ounces (150 gms)	2-3	1 gal (4 l)	2 tbsp	1 cup (250 ml)
1 pound (450 gms)	6-9	3 gals (12 l)	1/3 cup (75 ml)	3 cups (750 ml)

TIPS FOR MIXING YOUR DYE

If you already have a bottle mixed of the concentrated dye used for direct application, you can use this instead of dye powder. Use about 1/2 cup (125 ml) per gallon.

The most accurate way to figure out how much dye is needed is to weigh your fabric. However, I don't always have a scale handy, so instead I put my dry fabric into an empty bucket, estimate how much water will be needed, then follow the chart. If you are going to presoak your fabric, remember that wet fabric won't soak up as much liquid as dry fabric, so you'll need slightly less liquid. When in doubt, it's always better to mix more than less, so you don't need to scramble to add more dye once the soaking process has already begun.

The density of the color is related to the weight of the fabric, so the amount of water and the length of the dye bath won't affect the dye process in the ways you might expect. Using more dye than required for a color won't necessarily make that color darker; instead it may result in wasted dye and a longer washing-out process. A shorter dye bath will also result in more rinsing and wasted dye because the dyes haven't had a chance to properly bond with the fibers; to achieve a lighter color it is better to use less dye and leave it in the bath for the entire recommended time.

DYE POWDER (extra light)	DYE POWDER (light)	DYE POWDER (medium)	DYE POWDER (dark)	DYE POWDER (extra dark)
1/8 tsp	1/4 tsp	1/2 tsp	1 tsp	2 tsp
1/4 tsp	1/2 tsp	1 tsp	2 tsp	4 tsp
1/2 tsp	1 tsp	2 tsp	4 tsp	8 tsp
1 1/2 tsp	1 tbsp	2 tbsp	1/4 cup (60ml)	1/2 cup (125 ml)

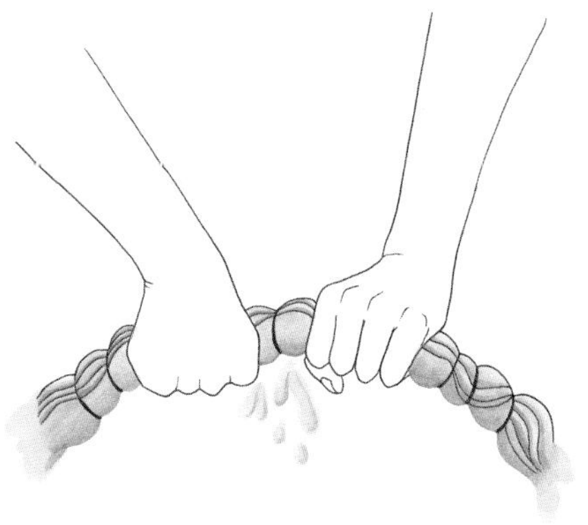

STEP 6. ADDING THE SODA ASH

While your fabric is soaking, dissolve the soda ash in a small amount of warm water. After the fabric has soaked for 15 minutes, lift the garment out of the bucket and add the soda ash mixture to the dye bath. Stir well, then place the garment back in the bath. Leave to soak for another hour, stirring occasionally throughout the process.

STEP 7. CURING

The best part about immersion dyeing is that you get to see the results right away! Instead of needing a long, additional curing process, the dye process itself serves as the curing period. Simply leave the garment soaking for a short period of time, usually about an hour depending on the effect and the color you are trying to achieve. As soon as you take it out of the dye bath you can wring it out, rinse, and wash.

STEP 8. THE REVEAL

Same as for direct application dyeing (page 59).

STEP 9. CLEANUP

STORAGE Because you've contaminated your dye bath with soda ash, you can't store it for later use, although your soda ash bath (if untainted by dye) can be stored and reused. If you want to reuse the dye bath immediately, it will still work for another batch or two, but keep in mind that the results may differ from your first bath as the dyes lose strength. Also, strangely enough, because dyeing is a chemical process, a tired blue dye bath won't necessarily yield a paler blue color; results can vary as widely as gold or purple or beige depending on the chemical makeup. (See page 42.)

DISPOSAL Same as for direct application dyeing (page 59).

CLEANING Same as for direct application dyeing (page 59).

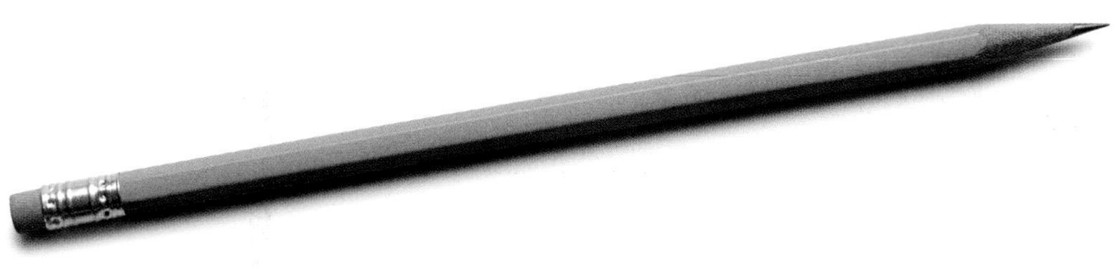

THE VARIABLE NATURE OF TIE-DYE

One of the most exciting things about tie-dye—its unpredictability—can also pose challenges. Many variables can alter your results: Fabric may take dyes differently based on the fiber content or weave, or even give different results from one fabric roll to the next. Dye results can vary based on manufacturer, production lot, amount used, and curing time. Even water temperature and humidity can change the results. I make samples for my clothing line in the winter and then go into production in the summer (or vice versa), so I often have to tweak my formulas to make up for the weather changes.

Because of this, it can be difficult to get the same results twice, or to replicate exactly a result that you see. Try not to worry too much about replicating things exactly, and welcome the surprises as they come. If you have a very specific color or pattern in mind, first test on the fabric you plan to use and take notes in order to try to re-create it later.

KEEPING NOTES

If you do choose to make tests and take notes, things I like to record are the date; fabric and fiber content; dye color and brand; quantity of dye, soda ash, additives, and water used; my tying and dyeing methods; curing time; and how I washed out the garment. If you test out a few colors or techniques at once, it's helpful to label them clearly so they're easy to differentiate after washing out. Marking them with a safety pin, stitch of thread, or waterproof marker is a good option.

I also like to keep notes on all of my tie-dye because you never know when a wonderful result will occur that you'll want to replicate.

That said, I encourage you to use the projects in this book as inspiration to try a variety of different dye methods and tying techniques. Expect to get unique results, enjoy the process, and embrace the unpredictability of the craft!

THERE'S MORE THAN ONE WAY TO PREPARE A DYE BATH

STANDARD METHOD

Added dry

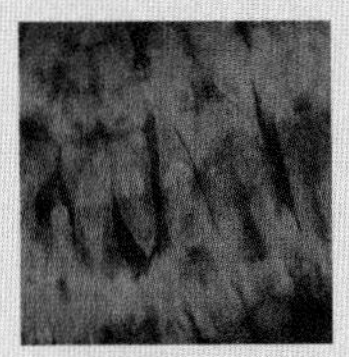

Added wet

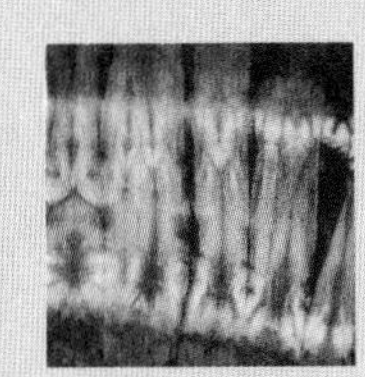

Added dry with salt

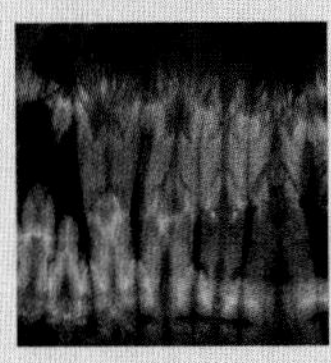

Added wet with salt

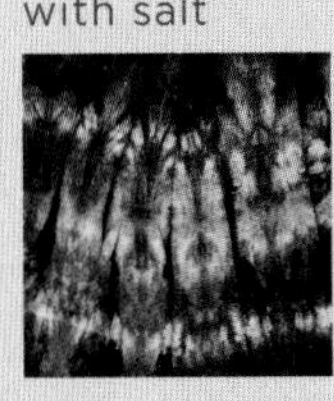

The standard immersion dye method, described in this chapter, has been formulated to create even color for solid dyeing, but since you're not trying to achieve uniform results in tie-dye, you may not feel the need to use this technique. Using the same dyes and additives, you can change the working order as described in the techniques that follow for a different experience and different results. You can skip the salt too if you don't mind getting a less saturated color. Results will vary with each technique.

PRESOAK METHOD

Added dry

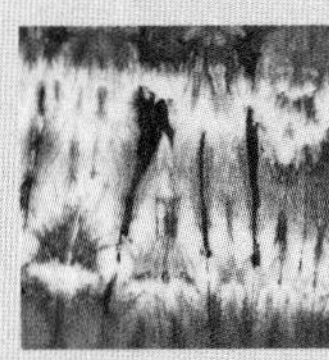

Added wet

Added dry with salt

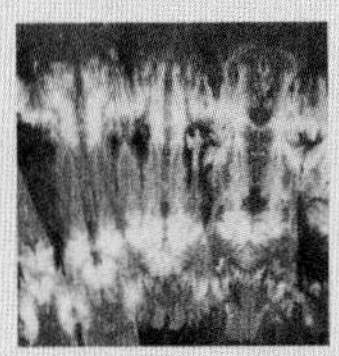

Added wet with salt

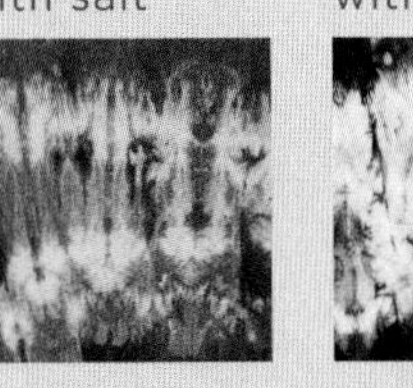

Try presoaking your garment in soda ash and then throw it into a dye bath following the same dye calculations as in the standard method (pages 62–63) but without the added soda ash. I often use this method if I already have a soda ash bath mixed and want to do a quick dye bath without the extra steps involved in the standard method. I also use it when I want a stronger contrast, since wetting the fabric before dyeing it causes the fabric to compress and create a suction that the dye has a harder time penetrating. Presoaking may yield slightly less intense colors than the standard method because the dye will begin to bond with the water before it has had a chance to fully saturate the fibers.

ALL-IN-ONE METHOD

Added dry

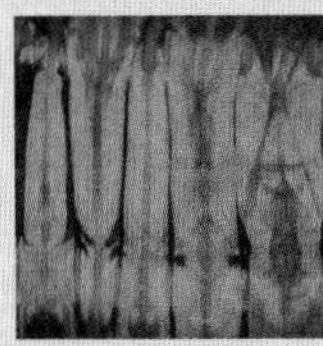

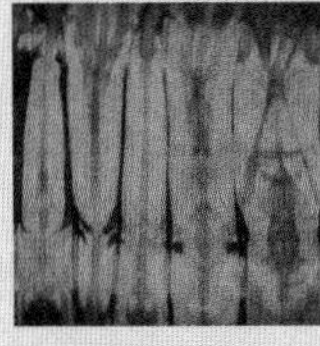

Added wet

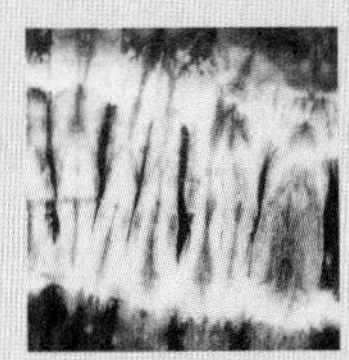

Added dry with salt

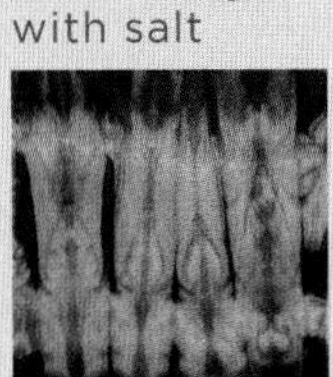

Added wet with salt

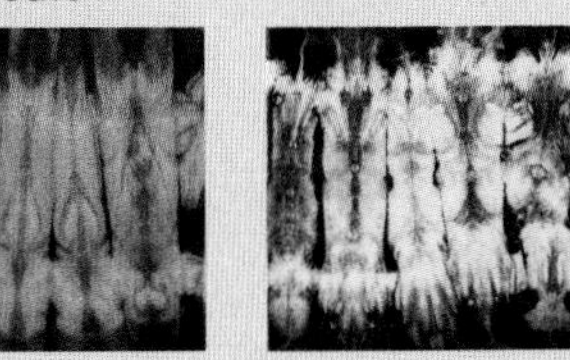

Without presoaking, use the same calculations as in the standard method (pages 62–63), and mix the dye, soda ash, and salt all together in the bath before adding your garments. This is the simplest method since everything is thrown into the bath at the same time, so I use it when I want to cut out those extra steps. I also use it when I want delicate shading and less contrast; if you immerse a dry garment, the dye generally penetrates further and more evenly than when immersing wet fabric, and offers more subtle variation in color and pattern. This method may also yield less intense colors.

ALTERNATIVE IMMERSION DYE METHODS

Immersion dye baths can be used in various ways. Try dyeing in multiple consecutive baths (see the Geode Skirt, page 76, and the Ripple Blanket, page 108), or try submerging only part of the garment in the dye. Dip your garment in a bath to create a sharp line (see the Dip-Dye Tote, page 144), or a gradated ombré effect (see the Ombré Day Gown, page 146). Or simply scrunch up your garment without using any string or rubber bands, then pour the dye over it, adding the minimum amount of dye mixture possible to submerge the fabric. Often the direct application dye mixture is used with this low-water immersion technique (see the Crystalline Scarf, page 84). With all of these variations, you can add the soda ash and dye in any sequence listed opposite.

ALTERNATIVE DIRECT APPLICATION METHODS

Using the same dye mixture, try other ways of applying the dye to a garment. Splatter, sprinkle, squirt, sponge, or spray (see the Mountain Peaks Tee, page 132). Dip the edge of a folded garment in a dish of dye (see the Classic Striped Tee, page 118). You can also use your dyes for stenciling, block printing, screen printing, batik, or hand-painting (see Watercolor Dress, page 140). Try combining techniques for even more varied effects.

THE PROJECTS

The best way to learn about tie-dye is to be hands on. So far, we've covered color, design, and the dyeing process. This chapter is where you'll put them to use, and where you'll actually experience the many tying and folding techniques available. You may be surprised to discover how many variations are possible even when using the same basic techniques. In the classes I teach, when ten students make the same project, we get ten different results, all of which are out-of-this-world beautiful!

In this chapter I will guide you through specific projects. Each project is designed to teach you something new. Feel free to go as you please. Even the more difficult projects are easy enough for a beginner; they just require a bit more time and preparation.

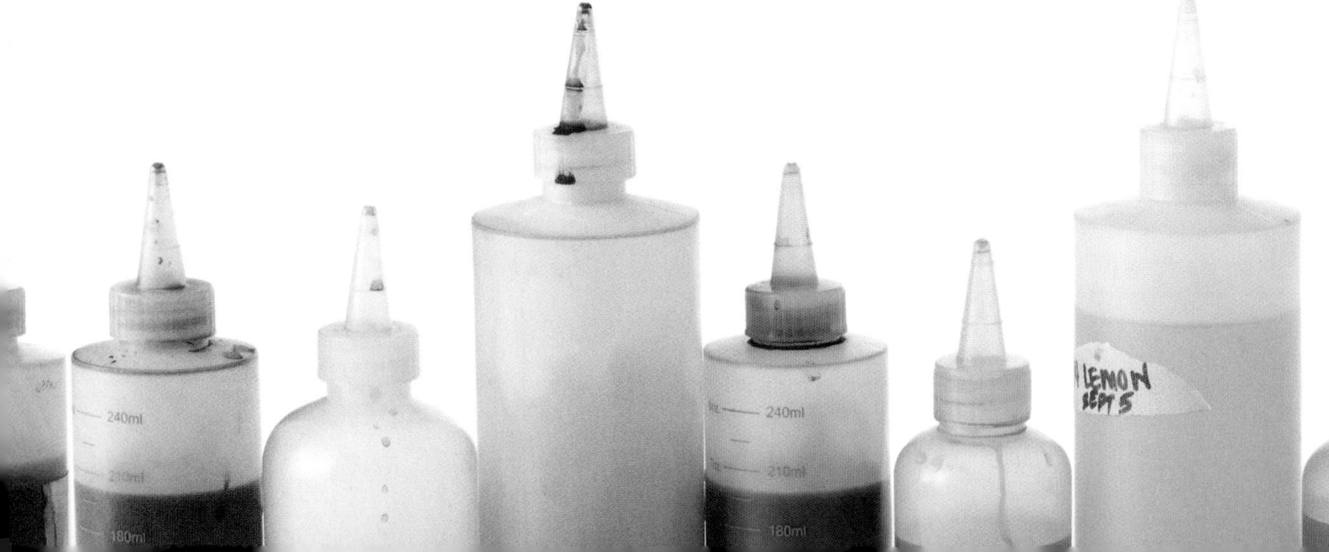

In the instructions, I give the fabrics and dyes that I used for each project. I do this to help you get started, but bear in mind that with tie-dye there is no exact formula; there are far too many variables (see page 65), so you shouldn't expect to get the exact same results I did. Always double-check the step-by-step instructions in the previous chapter as well as your product's mixing instructions, and then use your own judgment (for example, a small, thin T-shirt will use a lot less dye than a large, heavy sweatshirt). Experiment. Switch colors or try the same technique on a different fabric or garment. And remember what makes tie-dye so magical to begin with. Every creation is one-of-a-kind, and your results will be your own!

TYING PATTERNS

SCRUNCH

SCRUNCH

CIRCLES

CIRCLES

CIRCLES

STRIPES

STRIPES

STRIPES

FOLDING

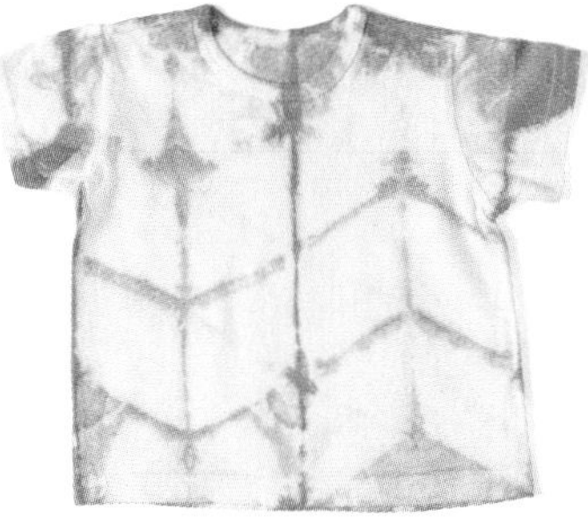

FOLDING

FOLDING

SCRUNCH

SCRUNCH

FOLDING & SCRUNCH

CIRCLES

SPIRALS

SPIRALS

FOLDING & STRIPES

KNOTTED

FOLDING

FOLDING

STITCHING

UNTIED

LIGHTNING TEE

This stunning design is surprisingly easy to do, and do well. The fabric simply has to be gathered and tied, but how you do it is up to you. Scrunch and tie the garment in a ball or flat for different effects. A flat disc of scrunched fabric will dye more evenly throughout, while a ball will result in areas of undyed fabric from the center of the ball and darker areas from the outside of the ball. Tie tightly to give another design effect; the white marks on these shirts are left behind by my criss-crossed rubber bands. And once you've tested it on a T-shirt, go ahead and use this technique to create spectacular effects on dresses, jackets, and bags. You'll find that once you've started, you won't want to stop!

LEVEL quick & easy

TIE METHOD scrunch

DYE METHOD immersion

CURING TIME 1 hour

TOOLS + MATERIALS

Off-white cotton T-shirt

Rubber bands

Fiber-reactive dye

Soda ash

Bucket

Measuring cup

Measuring spoons

Whisk

DYE COLOR

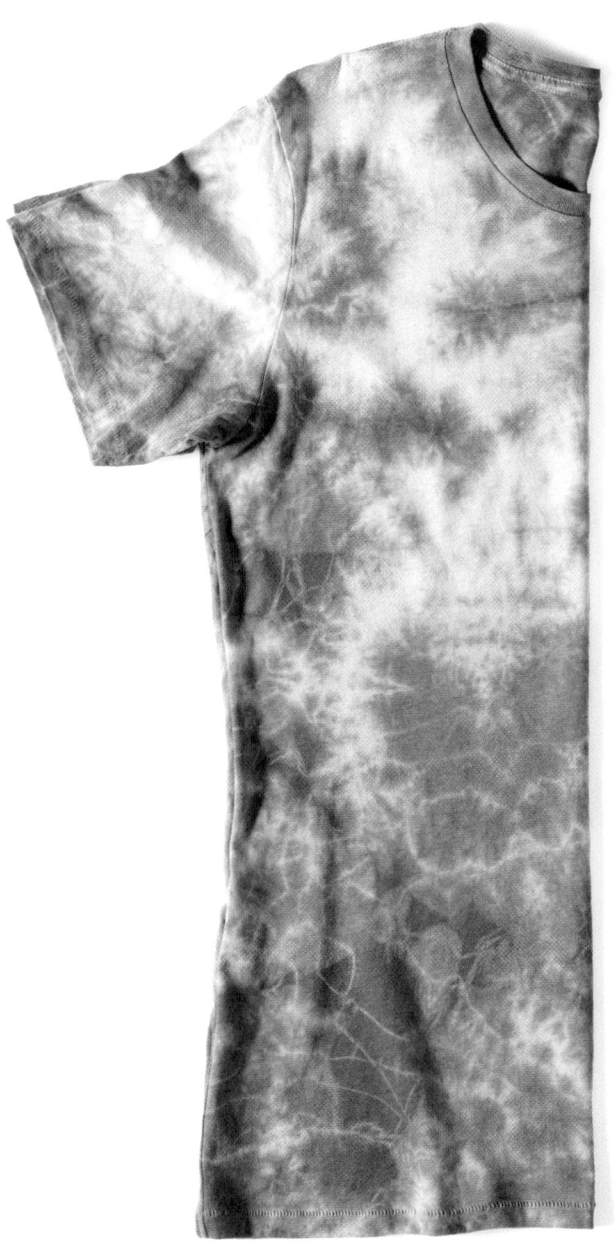

1. TIE

Gather a dry T-shirt in one large bundle and tie rubber bands around it. Tie the rubber bands fairly tightly, as in this method they will create a relief effect. Don't worry about whether the design is even; this project is all about the surprise.

2. PREP

Mix a dye bath, following the calculations for immersion dyeing on pages 62–63. Include the soda ash in the dye bath.

3. DYE + SET

Immerse the T-shirt in the dye bath and let it soak for 1 hour.

4. REVEAL

After the hour is up, rinse and wash as usual.

ALTERNATIVE *Presoak the T-shirt in soda ash before dyeing it to get more defined white areas (as pictured in the T-shirt below). The hue may change slightly as well depending on whether or not you presoak.*

TECHNIQUE: SCRUNCH

Scrunching is one of the most versatile methods of tie-dye and has the ability to be the most elegant. It's surprisingly also one of the simplest. Multiple bright colors can yield exciting results, or a subtle, refined look can be achieved by choosing a monochromatic palette or softer colors. You can scrunch the fabric when it is wet or dry, and dye it using either the bottle or immersion technique for equally stunning results. Tie tightly for more undyed areas or for immersion dyeing, and looser and flatter for fewer undyed areas or for bottle dyeing. Try combining this method with another, such as circles or stripes, or folding the garment before scrunching and see what sort of Rorschach test you get out of it. No matter what you do, you can't go wrong with scrunching.

GEODE SKIRT

The geode effect in this skirt is created by scrunching defined areas instead of scrunching the garment as a whole. Using this technique as a design element, you can tie up only part of the garment and leave the rest untied to create an interesting composition. I did this on the hem of this skirt, but you can try the shoulders of a shirt, a centered design, or whatever you dream up. You can also play around with color. In this project we will presoak the garment to create starker undyed areas, and dye it in multiple consecutive baths to create a richness of color beyond what you could achieve with just one dye bath.

LEVEL intermediate

TIE METHOD scrunch

DYE METHOD immersion

CURING TIME 1 hour

TOOLS + MATERIALS

- Off-white silk skirt
- Rubber bands
- Soda ash
- 4 buckets
- 3 colors of fiber-reactive dye
- Measuring cup
- Measuring spoons
- Whisk

DYE COLORS

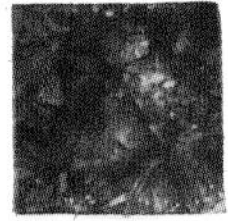

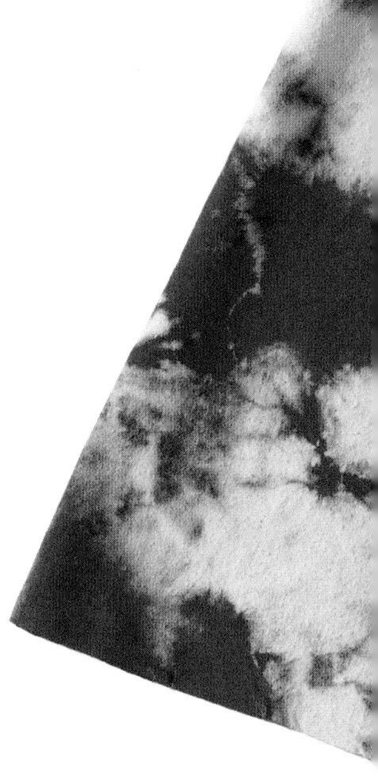

1. TIE

Beginning at the bottom of the skirt, grasp one area of the fabric and tie it up tightly with rubber bands. This time, instead of gathering the entire garment into one large bundle, grab multiple smaller, more distinct areas, and work with the skirt front and back as two separate layers. Repeat until the bottom half of the skirt is tied up (I had about 6 bundles); leave the top half of the skirt untied. The more random the better, so vary the size, placement, and amount of scrunch. Tie the rubber bands fairly tightly, as they will create a relief effect. Be sure not to make perfect circles; you are going for the organic look of a geode rock crystal that will come from pulling and scrunching randomly.

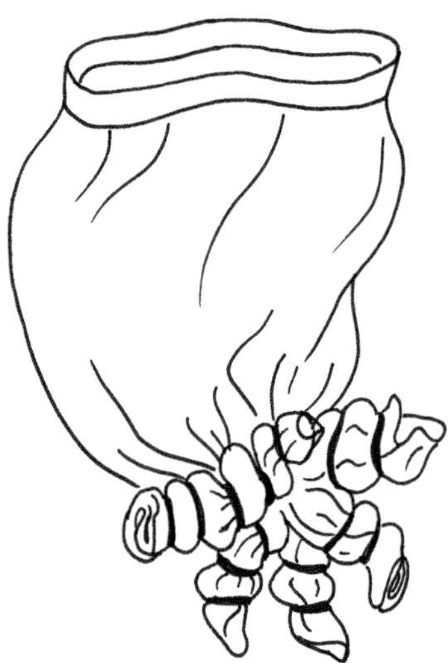

2. SET

Following the directions on page 54, presoak the skirt in soda ash for 30 minutes and wring out.

3. PREP

Choose 3 dye colors that will overlap nicely. While the skirt is presoaking, mix the first dye bath using your main color (I started with a reddish brown). Use the calculations for immersion dyeing (pages 62-63), skipping the soda ash since you are already presoaking.

4. DYE

Immerse the skirt in the dye bath. Dye for 20 minutes, stirring occasionally to ensure even coverage of the untied areas.

5. REPEAT

While the skirt is soaking in the first dye bath, mix the second dye bath in a separate bucket. It's often good to go darker on the second color (I used a dark blue). Wring out the skirt and immerse in the second dye bath. Dye for another 20 minutes, stirring often.

Repeat for the final bath (I used a gray to tone down the final results).

6. REVEAL

After the final dye bath, you will have dyed the skirt for a total of 1 hour; and can wring it out, then rinse and wash as usual.

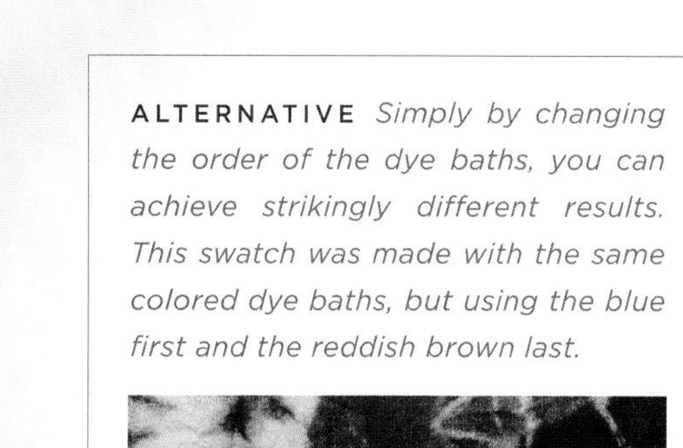

ALTERNATIVE *Simply by changing the order of the dye baths, you can achieve strikingly different results. This swatch was made with the same colored dye baths, but using the blue first and the reddish brown last.*

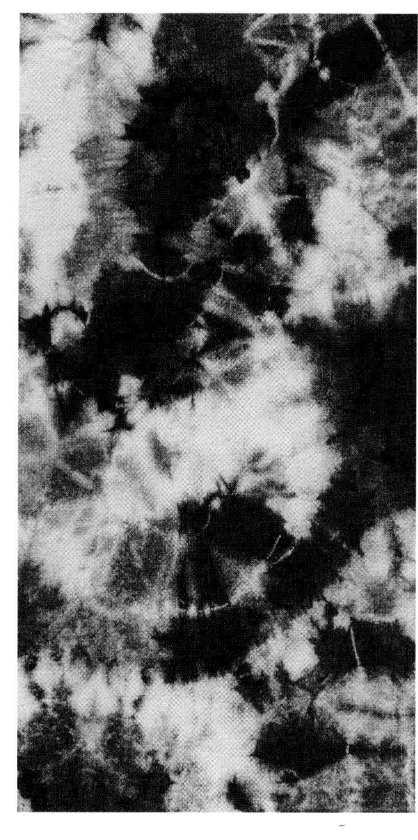

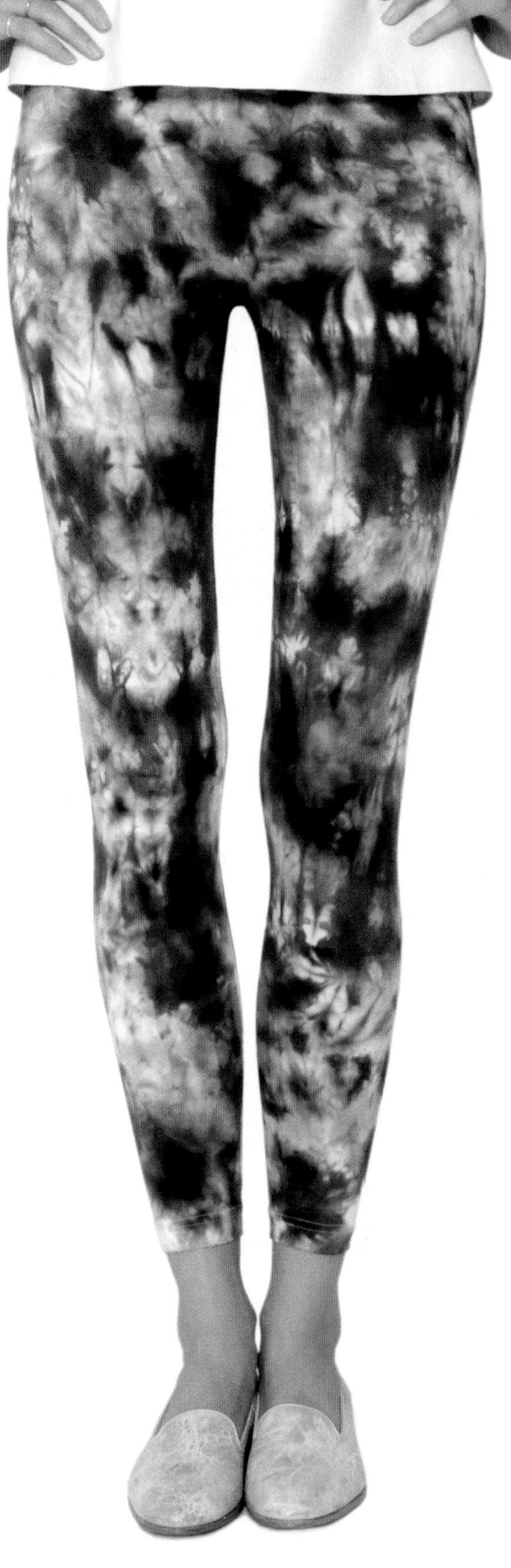

COSMIC LEGGINGS

These leggings are what got me started, both personally and professionally. Not only did I discover my love for tie-dye while creating them, but I got such great feedback every time I wore them out that I decided to start a clothing line! They are fun and colorful, but still flattering and wearable, I've made them in new colors every season since I launched my line. Use the colors that I suggest here or choose colors you love to wear and make them completely your own.

LEVEL beginner

TIE METHOD scrunch

DYE METHOD direct application

CURING TIME 24 hours

TOOLS + MATERIALS

White cotton leggings

Soda ash

Bucket

1–3 colors of fiber-reactive dye in similar hues for main colors

4–5 colors of fiber reactive dye in complementary hues for accent colors

5–8 squeeze bottles

Rubber bands

Old newspapers

Plastic bag

Measuring cup

Measuring spoons

Funnels

Whisk

MAIN DYE COLORS

ACCENT DYE COLORS

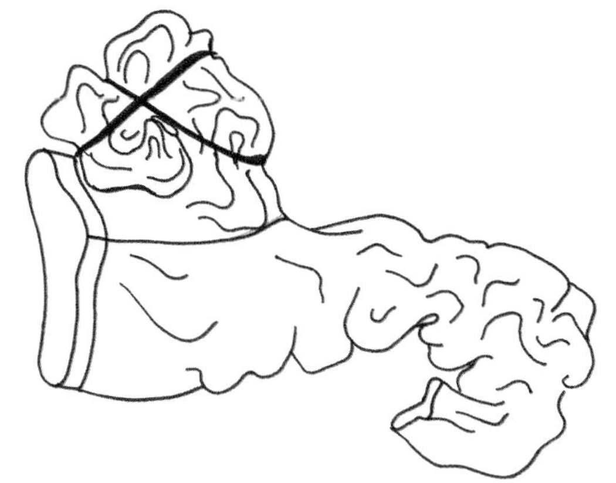

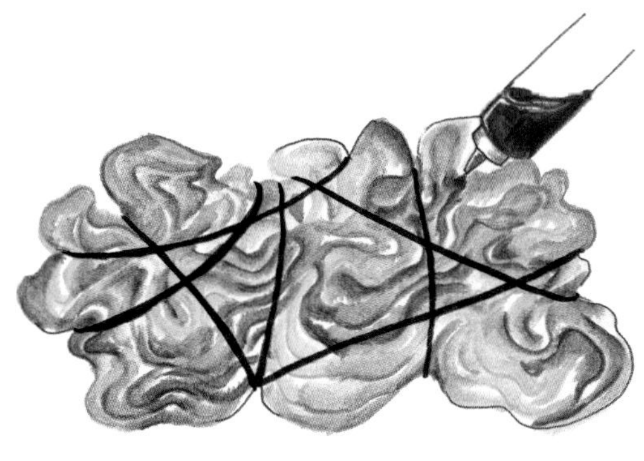

1. SET

Following the directions on page 54, presoak the leggings in soda ash for 30 minutes and wring out.

2. PREP

While the leggings are soaking, mix each dye color in an individual squeeze bottle (see page 56).

3. TIE

Lay the leggings on a clean work surface. Working with each leg separately, scrunch and gather areas of the fabric together, leaving the crotch visible so you can make sure that it is scrunched evenly and doesn't end up as a big undyed area.

Hold each gathered area together with overlapping rubber bands; 3 or 4 rubber bands placed in pie-shaped wedges work best. The rubber bands can be loose, as they are simply holding the scrunching in place.

TIP *While scrunching, try twirling or spiraling the fabric slightly to create movement in the finished design.*

4. DYE

Place the leggings on some newspaper to catch excess dye. Beginning with the accent colors, squeeze the dye deep inside the folds. Apply the colors one at a time, randomly over the entire area, until about half is covered in dye.

Apply the main color or colors in larger areas on the surface of the bundle until there is no white remaining. Leave dark colors for last, even if they are accent colors. Remember, there are always more undyed areas hiding between fabric folds than you think, so make sure to really saturate the fabric if you don't want any white on the leggings.

After you have fully saturated the first side, flip the leggings over and repeat on the second side.

5. CURE + REVEAL

Place the leggings in a plastic bag and leave for 24 hours, then rinse and wash as usual.

CRYSTALLINE SCARF

This technique, called space dyeing or low-water immersion dyeing, has the look of marbling (an incredibly difficult technique), but is much easier to do. You don't even need rubber bands—just scrunch up your scarf and pour dye over it. The variation in the depth of the color comes from the valleys of the fabric folds sitting in a puddle of dye while the peaks rise above.

LEVEL quick & easy

TIE METHOD scrunch

DYE METHOD direct application

CURING TIME 1 hour

TOOLS + MATERIALS

- White silk scarf
- Soda ash
- Bucket
- 3–5 colors of fiber-reactive dye
- 3–5 squeeze bottles
- Shallow container
- Measuring cup
- Measuring spoons
- Funnels
- Whisk

DYE COLORS

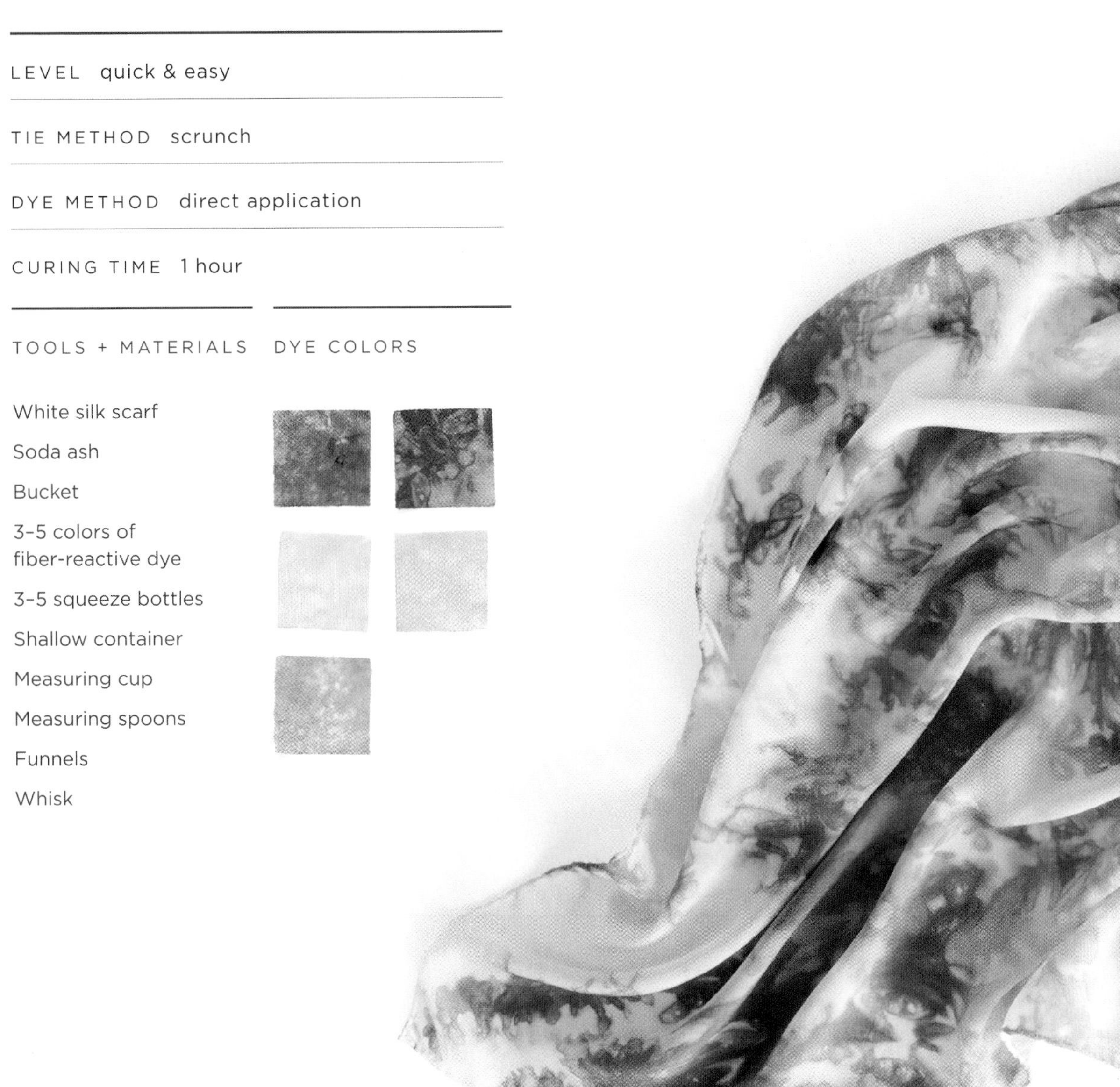

1. SET

Following the directions on page 54, presoak the scarf in soda ash for 30 minutes and wring out.

2. PREP

While the scarf is soaking, mix each dye color in an individual squeeze bottle, using the calculations for direct application (page 56).

3. TIE

Scrunch the scarf in one loose layer inside a shallow container so that the fabric is crumpled but not folded over entirely.

4. DYE

Remove the nozzles of the squeeze bottles and pour the dye over large swaths of the fabric. Apply the dye one color at a time, overlapping in some areas.

TIP *For another effect, try sprinkling rock salt on top of your fabric as you apply the dye. The salt will attract the moisture and create interesting patterns.*

5. CURE + REVEAL

Wait 1 hour. If you prefer, you can cover the scarf loosely with plastic and leave it for up to 24 hours; the longer you wait, the more the colors will blend together. Rinse and wash as usual.

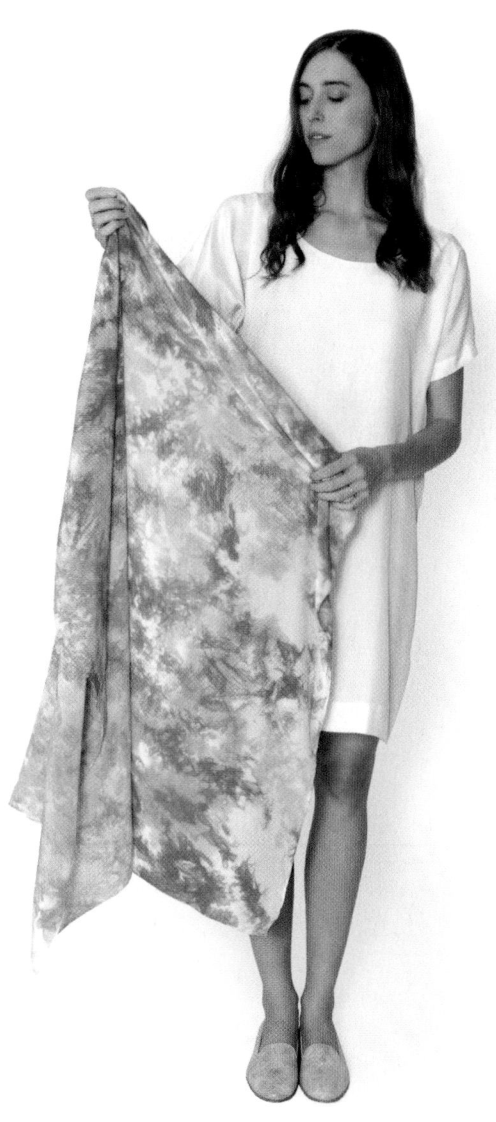

ALTERNATIVE Another form of low-water immersion dyeing, often called jelly jar dyeing, involves scrunching the fabric tightly into a container, then filling it with dye. Quilters often use this method to make monochromatic yet textured fabrics for their projects.

With both methods, you can start with either presoaked or dry fabric, and add the soda ash with the dye or after the dye. Each variation will offer its own unique results.

CIRCLE PILLOWS

For these pillows, I made three variations on the circle: a ring, a bull's-eye, and a spider-web. The technique is simple and the variations are made using small changes with dramatic results. The circle is elegant on its own, but you can also use it as a design element, varying the size, placement, or quantity to create a more complex composition.

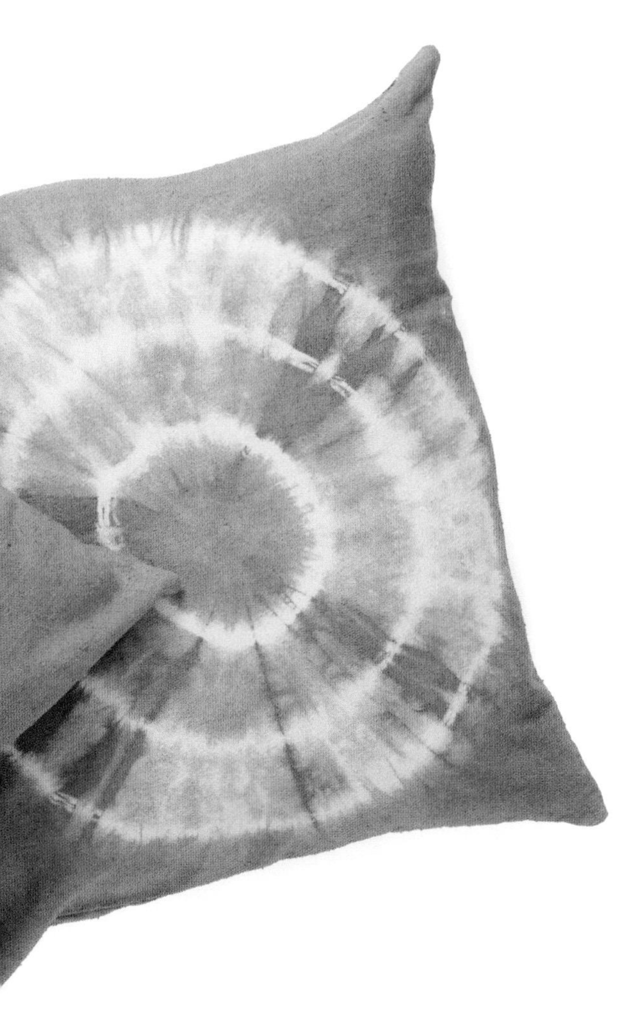

LEVEL beginner

TIE METHOD circles

DYE METHOD immersion

CURING TIME 1 hour

TOOLS + MATERIALS

3 off-white square silk pillowcases

Soda ash

2 buckets

Fiber-reactive dye

Rubber bands

Measuring cup

Measuring spoons

Whisk

DYE COLOR

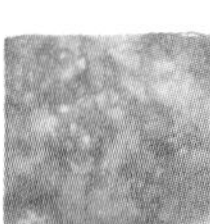

1. SET

Following the directions on page 54, presoak the pillowcases in soda ash for 30 minutes and wring out.

2. PREP

While the pillowcases are presoaking, mix a dye bath using the calculations for immersion dyeing (pages 62–63), skipping the soda ash since you are already presoaking.

RING

BULL'S-EYE

SPIDERWEB

3. TIE

FOR THE RING Lay the first pillowcase flat on the table. Working only with the top layer, pinch the center of the fabric and pull away from the bottom layer and up into a long, narrow bundle with the center as the tip. You can even out the folds or leave them random depending on the look you're going for.

Tie a rubber band 2–3" (5–7.5 cm) above the edges of the pillowcase, binding tightly. Loosen the fabric inside the ring, forming a balloon. The corners of the pillowcase will stick out farther than the flat edges. If you want a thicker, more solid circle, add overlapping rubber bands to ensure a decent relief area.

Leave the corners, edges, and back of the pillow unbound so that they will dye solid.

FOR THE BULL'S-EYE Again, working from the center and only using the top layer of fabric, pull the pillowcase up into a narrow bundle. This time starting at the tip, tie a rubber band about an inch (2.5 cm) down, binding tightly.

Continue to tie rubber bands at intervals farther down the length of the fabric. You can tie them in even increments or more randomly, and as close or far away as you'd like your concentric circles to be. The closer they are to each other, the harder it will be for the dye to penetrate and the more white areas you will have. Finish tying the rubber bands about 2" (5 cm) from the edge of the pillow, again leaving the corners, edges, and back of the pillow unbound.

FOR THE SPIDERWEB Pulling the pillowcase up in the same manner, take one rubber band and tie it around the first few inches (approximately 7.5 cm) of the tip tightly but open and spread out, rather than in one place like you did on the ring and bull's-eye. Repeat with more rubber bands, overlapping and creating a continuous wrapping until you reach the base of the bundle, again leaving the corners, edges, and back loose. The closer and tighter you wrap, the more white areas you will have. You can use string instead of rubber bands if you prefer.

4. DYE

Immerse the pillowcases in the dye bath and let them soak for an hour.

5. REVEAL

After the hour is up, rinse and wash as usual.

> **ALTERNATIVE** *If you want the design to show through on both sides, pinch both sides together and wrap them as one.*

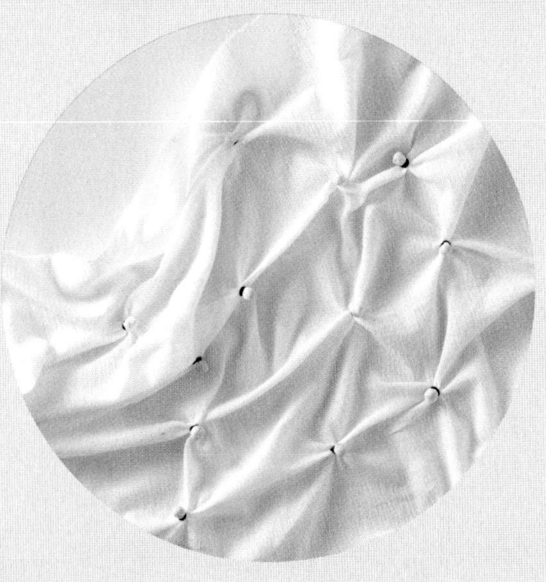

TECHNIQUE: CIRCLES

Circles are especially fun to use because the results can vary so widely. Using the circle as a basic building block of design, you can play with the idea of size, repetition, layout, and precision (or lack thereof).

This technique's myriad uses have been explored for centuries. The tradition in Central Asia is to create simple, orderly grids of rings, while Berber artists in Morocco and Tunisia create free-form designs. Indian saris display elaborate patterns made up of minuscule circles, while in West Africa they enlarge the circles to make graphic, oversized motifs. Use these ideas as inspiration to see how far you can take this technique.

Simple, everyday objects have always been used to create circles. In Morocco, date pits are tied inside each circle. In Africa, they use objects such as shells and stones. Specialized tools have been invented all over the world to help create circle or dot patterns. In India and Indonesia a bed of nails was once used to mark a pattern on the fabric before tying it; these days the pattern is printed onto the fabric first. In India, long fingernails or a special pointed ring are used to hook the fabric. In Indonesia, a pointed tool does the trick and in Japan, engineered hooks attached to a workbench help speed up the process—you would be amazed at how quickly hundreds of tiny tied circles can be made!

POLKA-DOT DRESS

This project is a little time consuming, but the results are worth it. To make circles of the same size and shape, tie objects such as marbles, buttons, rice, or beans inside each point. If you want your polka dots to be less uniform, you can tie them without anything inside. Plot out a design or do it free-form. If you want to take this in another direction, you can use any of the types of circles you learned in the previous project and repeat them as your polka dots.

TIP *I wanted this dress to be a true, strong black, which can often be hard to achieve. In order to do so, I used the standard immersion dye method and added salt, but you can use any immersion method on page 66 and skip the salt if you decide on a different color.*

LEVEL intermediate

TIE METHOD circles

DYE METHOD immersion

CURING TIME 1 hour

TOOLS + MATERIALS

White cotton dress

Chalk or fabric marker

Small dried beans or beads to tie inside each circle (I used mung beans, which are about 1/8"–1/4" [3–6mm] in diameter)

Rubber bands

Plastic wrap, cut into small pieces

Fiber-reactive dye

Salt

Bucket

Soda ash

Measuring cup

Measuring spoons

Whisk

DYE COLOR

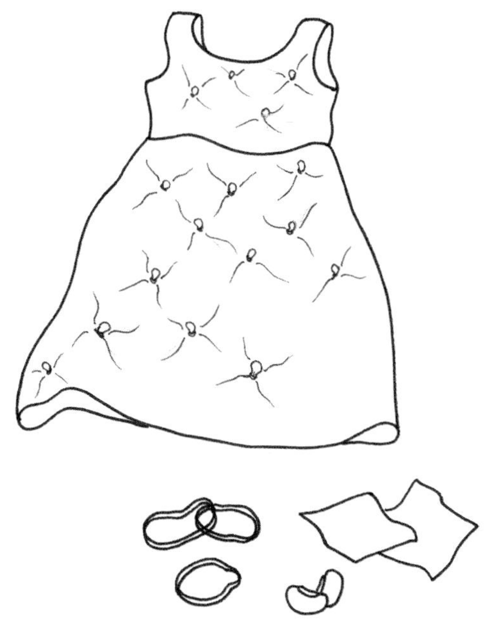

1. TIE

Working with a dry dress, lay it flat on your work space and plot out your design, marking areas where you want polka dots with chalk, with each mark indicating the center of a dot.

Beginning with the first mark, place a bean underneath the fabric and grasp it from above. Place a piece of plastic wrap on top of the fabric, then wrap a rubber band around the plastic wrap and fabric, securing the bean inside. Repeat for the remaining polka dots.

2. PREP

Mix a dye bath using the standard immersion dye method (pages 62–63) to achieve even coverage on the untied areas. Dissolve the salt in some hot water and add to the bath before immersing your dress. Mix the soda ash mixture separately, setting it aside to add later. Make sure that all of the water you use in your different mixtures equals the total amount that you need.

3. DYE

Wet the dress in plain water so that it is fully and evenly saturated, then wring out. Immerse it in the dye bath and stir for 15 minutes to ensure even coverage on the untied areas.

4. SET

After 15 minutes, lift the dress out of the bucket and add the soda ash mixture to the dye bath. Stir well, then place the dress back in the dye. Let soak for an hour, stirring occasionally.

5. REVEAL

After the hour is up, rinse and wash as usual.

> **ALTERNATIVE** *For another effect, try dyeing the fabric in the first bath, then removing some of the rubber bands or adding new ones, and dyeing it in a bath of a second color.*

ALTERNATIVE *If you want just the outline of the circle with a dyed center, skip the plastic wrap and follow the same instructions.*

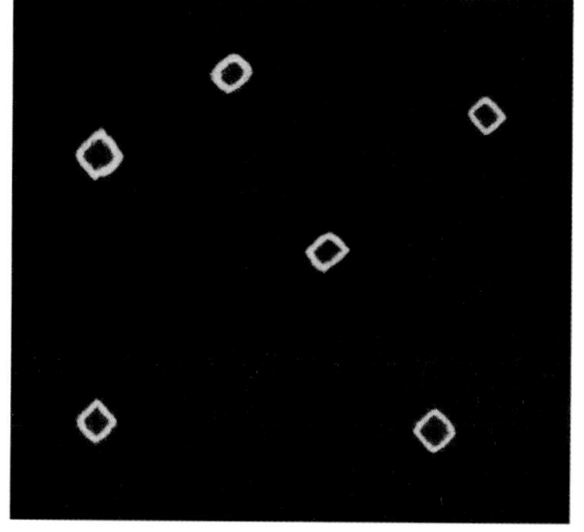

SPIRAL TEES

This is one of the tying techniques where your dye application can have the biggest impact on the final results. Even when tying the same way and using the same colors, it's possible to get vastly different results depending on how you apply the dye.

LEVEL beginner

TIE METHOD spirals

DYE METHOD direct application

CURING TIME 24 hours

TOOLS + MATERIALS

4 white cotton T-shirts

Soda ash

Bucket

3 colors of fiber-reactive dye

Squeeze bottles

Rubber bands

Old newspapers

Plastic bags

Measuring cup

Measuring spoons

Funnels

Whisk

DYE COLORS

1. SET

Following the directions on page 54, presoak the T-shirts in soda ash for 30 minutes and wring out.

2. PREP

While the T-shirts are soaking, mix 3 colors of dye in individual squeeze bottles (see page 56).

3. TIE

Lay the T-shirts out flat on a clean work space. For this project, you will be tying all four shirts exactly the same way. Find the center point for the spiral, which should be in line with the armpits of the shirt rather than the actual center. This will draw the eye up toward the face and away from the belly.

Pinching with your fingers or using a tool such as a chopstick or a fork, press down on the center point and begin to spiral the fabric either clockwise or counterclockwise. Lead the loose fabric with your other hand, gathering the folds evenly and keeping them all about the same height, creating a fairly even, flat disc. Continue twisting the fabric until it is all gathered together in one spiraled disc.

On each T-shirt, use 3 rubber bands to hold it together loosely, creating 6 pie-shaped wedges.

4. DYE

Place the T-shirts on some newspaper to catch excess dye. Using the same 3 colors, you will apply the dye differently on each shirt.

RANDOM Apply the colors randomly as you did with the Cosmic Leggings (page 81), squeezing the dye in between the folds and making sure to fully saturate the fabric. Flip the shirt over and repeat on the second side.

CONCENTRIC CIRCLES Starting in the center, apply the dyes in concentric circles, making sure that colors placed next to each other will look good where they overlap. Squeeze the dye deep inside the folds, then flip the shirt over to dye the second side, applying the dye in the same areas on both sides.

PIE-SHAPED WEDGES Using the rubber bands as guidelines, divide the bundle into 3 sections, each containing 2 neighboring wedges. Apply a different dye in each of the 3 sections. Flip over and repeat, applying the dye in the same areas on both sides.

OFFSET Apply 1 color to the entire first side, saturating the surface well. Flip the shirt over and dye the entire second side another color. Because each side represents either a hill or a valley in the folds of the T-shirt, the two colors will form two offset, interlinked spirals, like alternating stripes radiating from the center of the shirt.

TIP *This dyeing method creates exciting results if you dye one side multicolored and the second side a solid color such as black or gray.*

5. CURE + REVEAL

Place each T-shirt inside its own plastic bag and leave for 24 hours, then rinse and wash as usual.

RANDOM

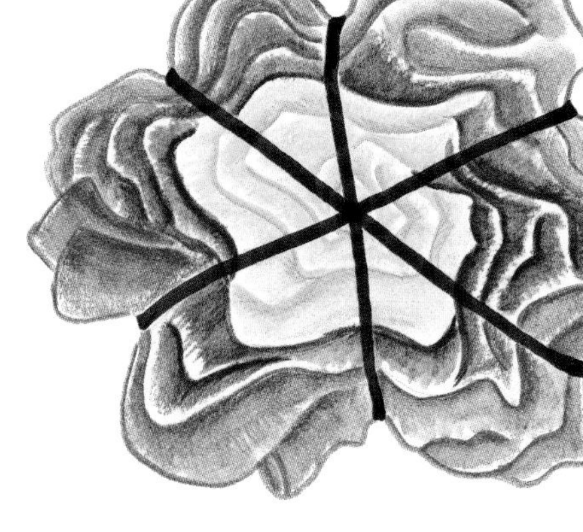

CONCENTRIC

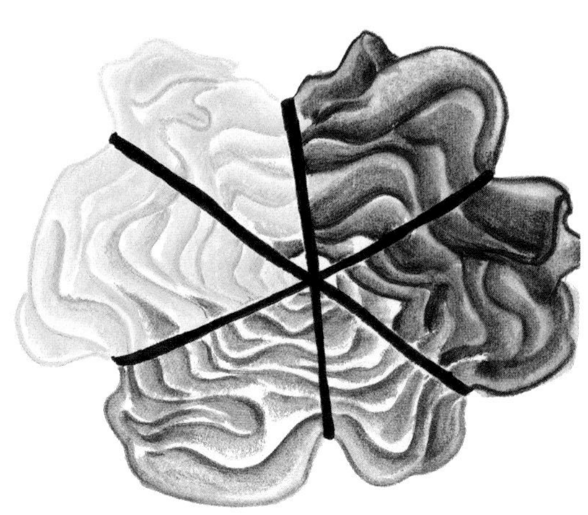

PIE-SHAPED

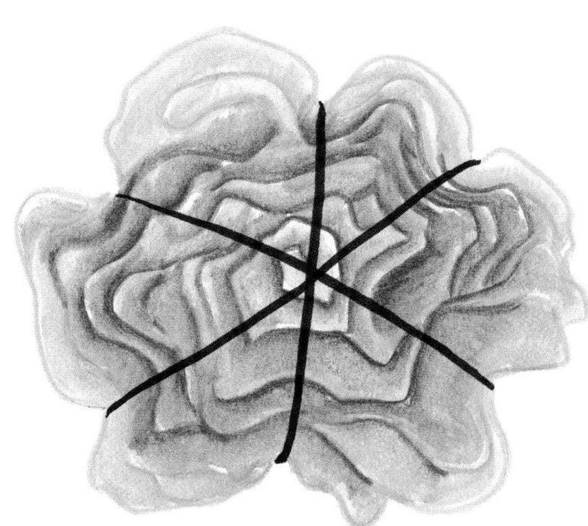

OFFSET

DOUBLE TWIST DRESS

Spirals can be a wonderful way to create flowing movement in a design, but they don't have to look as recognizable as the iconic spiral design of the sixties. Try positioning the center of the spiral in an unexpected place, like the shoulder or hem. By placing it toward an edge of the garment, you will achieve the movement of the spiral without it being too obvious. For a less distinct spiral, twist looser and messier, and don't worry about gathering the fabric evenly. Using the spiral in these ways can elevate it to a new level, one that is more unexpected and elegant.

LEVEL beginner

TIE METHOD spirals

DYE METHOD direct application

CURING TIME 6 hours

TOOLS + MATERIALS

Off-white silk dress
Soda ash
Bucket
3 colors of fiber-reactive dye
Squeeze bottles
Rubber bands
Old newspapers
Plastic bag
Measuring cup
Measuring spoons
Funnels
Whisk

DYE COLORS

1. SET

Following the directions on page 54, presoak the dress in soda ash for 30 minutes and wring out.

2. PREP

While the dress is soaking, mix 3 colors of dye in individual squeeze bottles (see page 56).

3. TIE

Lay the dress flat on a clean work space. Choose a spot on the left side of the dress toward the top as the center of the first spiral and turn counterclockwise, keeping the bundle fairly flat and the hills and valleys even. Use most of the fabric of the dress in this spiral.

Find a spot on the right side of the dress toward the bottom hem as the center of a second spiral and turn clockwise, pulling the remainder of the available fabric into this spiral.

Hold each gathered area together with overlapping rubber bands as you did with the Cosmic Leggings (page 81).

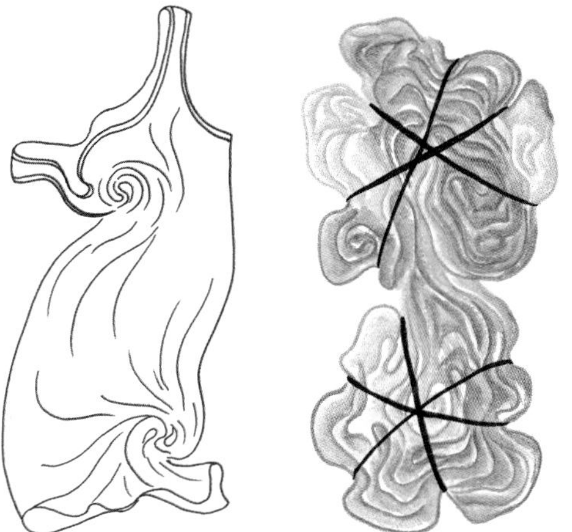

4. DYE

Place the dress on some newspaper to catch excess dye. Remove the nozzles of the squeeze bottles and pour the dye over large areas of the spirals. Apply the dye randomly, one color at a time, overlapping in some areas.

Flip the dress over and apply to the other side, without worrying about applying the colors in the same areas as the first side.

5. CURE + REVEAL

Place the dress inside a plastic bag and leave for 6 hours, then rinse and wash as usual.

TECHNIQUE: SPIRALS

Perhaps the most iconic of the American tie-dye techniques, the spiral can be used in full rainbow force or manipulated and used as a subtler design element, again playing with size, placement, repetition, and color choice. It can also be combined with other effects such as folding or scrunching to create interesting twists on the classic spiral.

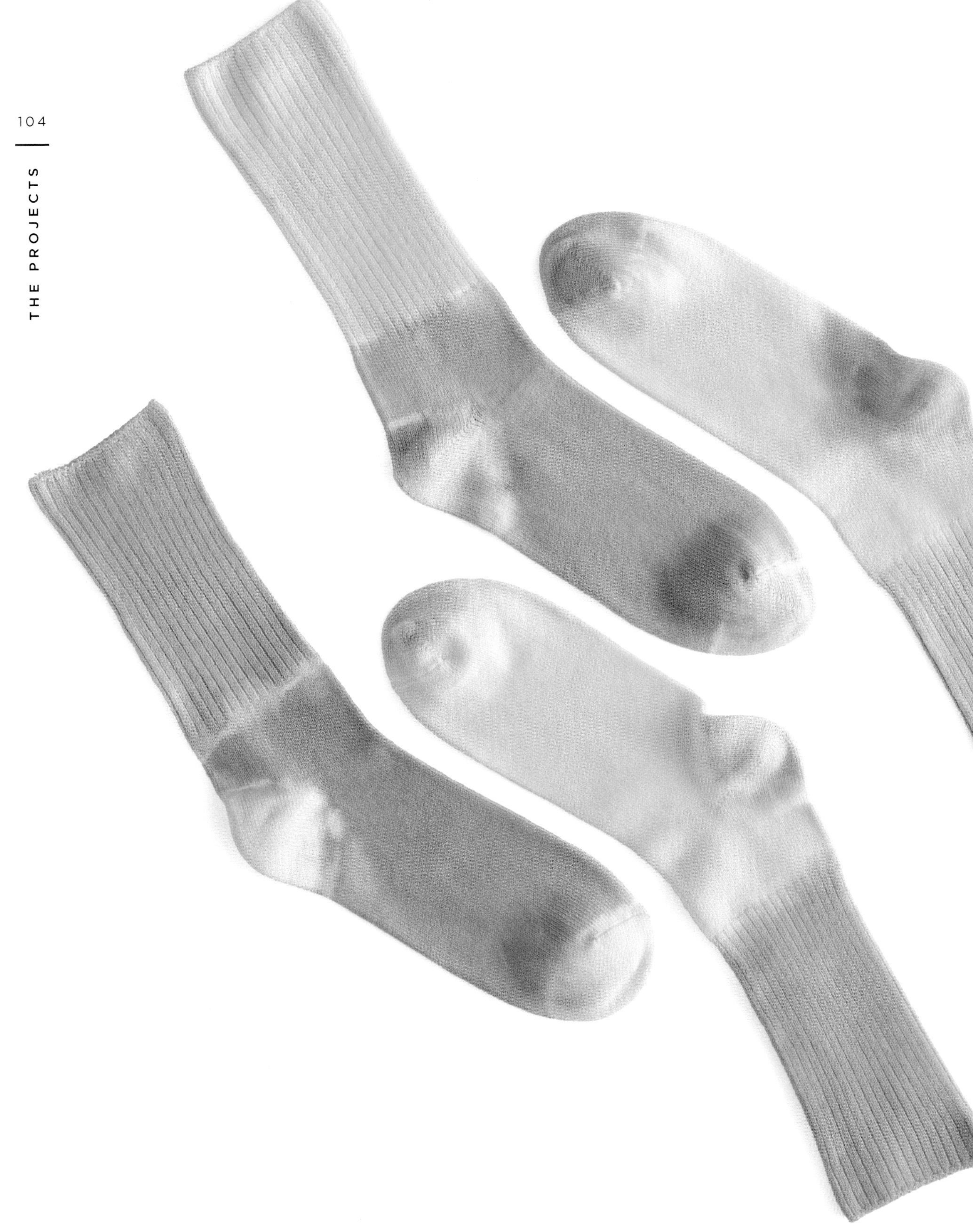

COLOR-BLOCKED SOCKS

These bold, color-blocked socks are easy to make and fun to wear. By tying the rubber bands tightly, we create defined white lines, and by using them as guides, we take a second approach and dye bold colorful stripes. When tying rubber bands tightly to create relief stripes, there is often feathering in the opposite direction as a result of the gathering. If you want to avoid the feathering, fully saturate the folds around the rubber bands, otherwise embrace this innate quality for its imperfect beauty.

LEVEL beginner

TIE METHOD stripes

DYE METHOD direct application

CURING TIME 24 hours

TOOLS + MATERIALS

White cotton or bamboo rayon socks

Soda ash

Bucket

3 colors of fiber-reactive dye

3 squeeze bottles

Rubber bands

Old newspapers

Plastic bag or plastic wrap

Measuring cup

Measuring spoons

Funnels

Whisk

DYE COLORS

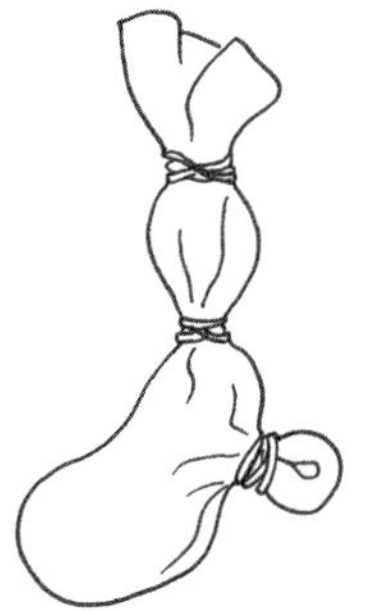

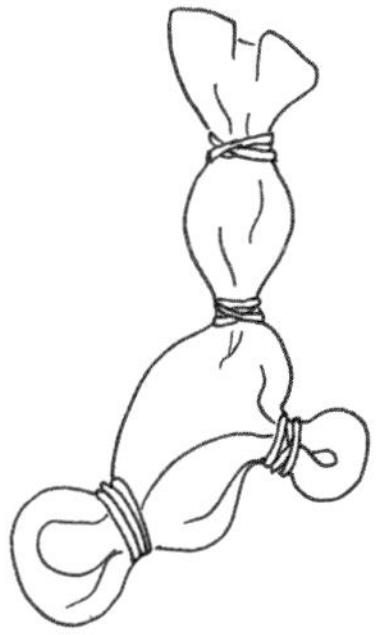

1. SET

Following the directions on page 54, presoak the socks in soda ash for 30 minutes and wring out.

2. PREP

While the socks are soaking, mix 3 colors of dye in individual squeeze bottles (see page 56).

3. TIE

Lay the socks flat on a clean work space. Working with the first sock, tie rubber bands horizontally around the ankle wherever you want white stripes, then tie the heel and toe in separate sections. For fully striped socks, continue the parallel bands all the way down to the toe instead of tying the heel and toe separately. Repeat with the second sock, making sure to align the stripes with the first one.

4. DYE

Place the socks on some newspaper to catch any excess dye during the dye process. Apply each color, one at a time, to the areas in between the rubber bands. Make sure to get inside the folds. Stop just before reaching the rubber band, as the dyes will bleed further and colors will blend where they touch. Flip the socks over and repeat on the other side.

5. CURE + REVEAL

To avoid having the colors rub off on each other in the plastic bag, roll the socks up in a newspaper before placing them inside the bag, or simply leave them flat on the table and cover in plastic while they cure. Leave for 24 hours, then rinse and wash as usual.

ALTERNATIVE: *For a classic, French-inspired striped garment, tie it the same way and then throw it in an immersion bath to dye it a solid color.*

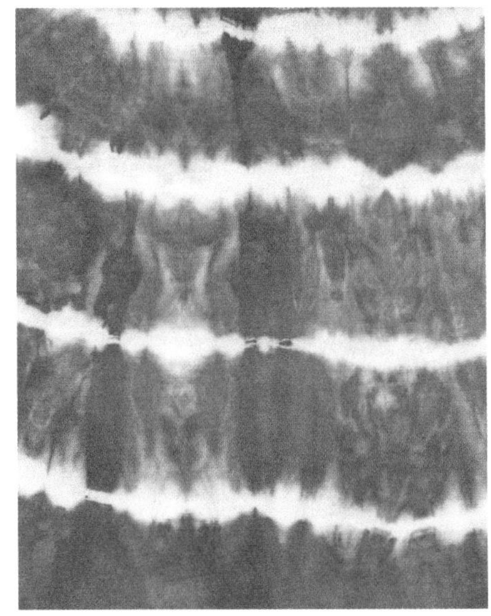

TECHNIQUE: STRIPES

Stripes can be bold and fun, like a classic French sailor shirt, or can be used to create a more organic and delicate look. A striped pattern can come from a variety of sources: gathering or folding the fabric, a relief pattern created by rubber bands or thread, or the application of the dye itself. Sometimes one of these methods will work alone, but often you will see them working together—subtle striping from the folds in one direction, with stark relief from the rubber bands in the other direction. Simple design choices such as placement, scale, and color will make all the difference and open up a world of possibilities. With time and experience you will begin to understand how to control these, but the results of even first-time trials are always stunning and fun.

RIPPLE BLANKET

For this blanket, we will create stripes that are less defined and more organic. By gathering in small, uneven pleats and binding tightly, you can create wonderful striping with an unexpected level of sophistication. The main stripes are the edges of the pleats exposed to the dye, but if you look closely within those areas, you will see that traces left behind by your string or rubber bands have also created wonderful striping in the opposite direction.

LEVEL intermediate

TIE METHOD stripes

DYE METHOD immersion

CURING TIME 1 hour

TOOLS + MATERIALS

- White cotton blanket
- String
- Soda ash
- 3 buckets
- 2 colors of fiber-reactive dye
- Measuring cup
- Measuring spoons
- Whisk

DYE COLORS

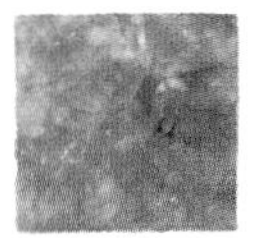

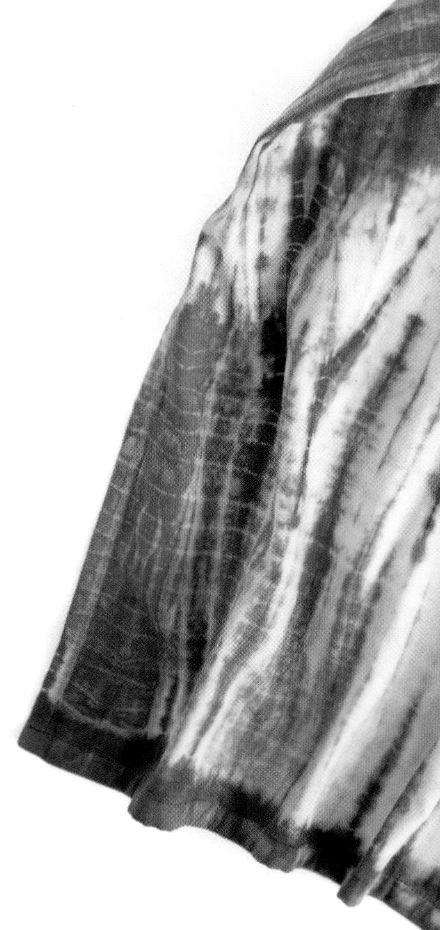

1. TIE

First, cut a piece of string approximately seven times the length of your blanket and make a slipknot at one end. Starting with one side of the blanket, gather the fabric together horizontally in small, loose, even pleats. Slide the slipknot around the pleats and pull tightly. Take the long end of the string and begin to wrap it around the fabric to hold the pleats in place. Keep wrapping along the length of the blanket, forming a long, fat rope, and rearranging the fabric every few inches (approximately every 10 cm) to ensure continuity in the pleats. They don't have to be perfect, but it's important to make sure that the ridges of the pleats are visible at the top and bottom of the rope because the visible areas will become your dyed stripes while the hidden areas will remain white. The tighter and closer you wrap, the more white areas you will have in the final design.

2. SET

Following the directions on page 54, presoak the blanket in soda ash for 30 minutes and wring out.

3. PREP

While the blanket is presoaking, choose your main color and mix the first dye bath (I started with gray). Use the calculations for immersion dyeing (pages 62–63), skipping the soda ash since you are already presoaking.

4. DYE

Immerse the blanket in the dye bath and let it soak for 30 minutes, stirring occasionally.

5. REPEAT

While the blanket is soaking in the first dye bath, mix the second dye bath the same way. You want to choose a color that will overlap nicely with the first. Keep in mind that darker colors may overwhelm lighter ones. Wring out the blanket and immerse it in the second dye bath for another 30 minutes.

6. REVEAL

After the second dye bath, you will have dyed the blanket for a total of 1 hour; now you can wring it out, then rinse and wash as usual.

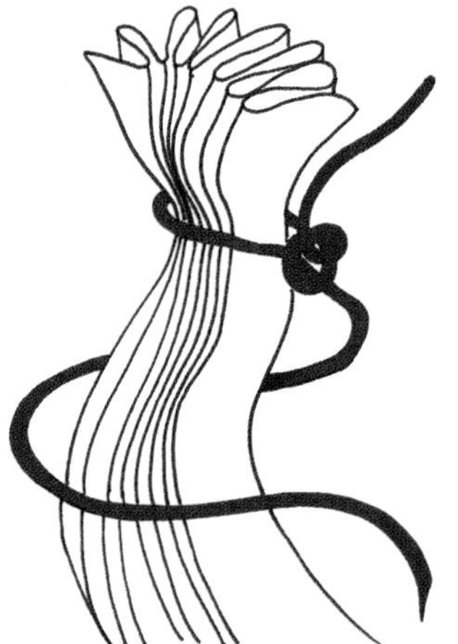

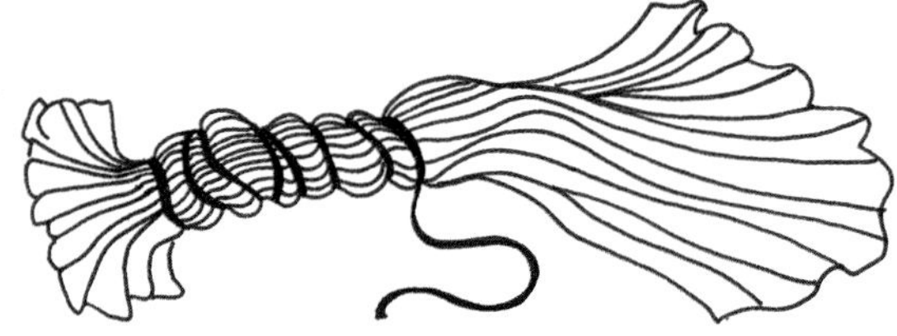

SUNSHINE TUNIC

To create this chevron stripe, we will combine the striping technique of the last project with a simple center fold that produces a bold mirrored effect. By arranging the stripe in a diagonal and tying only part of the garment, we allow the remainder of the garment to dye a solid color and produce striking results.

LEVEL intermediate

TIE METHOD folding and stripes

DYE METHOD immersion

CURING TIME 1 hour

TOOLS + MATERIALS

White silk tunic

Rubber bands

Soda ash

2 buckets

Fiber-reactive dye

Measuring cup

Measuring spoons

Whisk

DYE COLOR

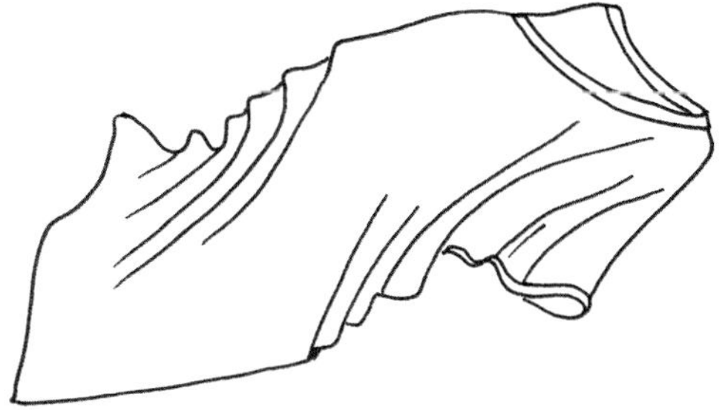

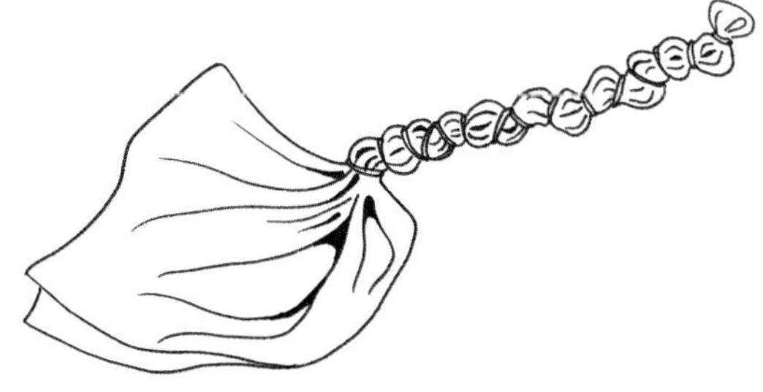

1. TIE

Lay the tunic flat on a clean work space with the back facing up. Fold it in half lengthwise down the center, with the back on the inside of the fold. Find the top of the V near the armpit, and the bottom of the V near the waistline, and draw an imaginary line between the two points. Gather the material along that line and slide a rubber band around the fabric, tying tightly.

Gather the material above the first rubber band in loose pleats and wrap with another rubber band, tightly but open and spread out. Repeat with more rubber bands, overlapping continuously until you reach the top, leaving everything below the first rubber band unwrapped to dye solid. The tighter and closer you wrap the rubber bands, the more white areas you will have in your design.

2. SET

Following the directions on page 54, presoak the tunic in soda ash for 30 minutes and wring out.

3. PREP

While the tunic is presoaking, mix the dye bath. Use the calculations for immersion dyeing (pages 62–63), skipping the soda ash since you are already presoaking.

4. DYE

Immerse the tunic in the dye bath and let it soak for an hour, stirring occasionally and making sure that the untied area is getting fully and evenly saturated.

5. REVEAL

After the hour is up, rinse and wash as usual.

ALTERNATIVE *This simple center-folding technique can be combined with any of the tying techniques to create a mirrored effect.*

INDIGO BUTTON-DOWN

Another extremely simple tying method is knotting the fabric itself. This method creates a gathered effect with faint striping where the fabric turns in on itself. It produces a wonderfully subtle effect and is great for any garment or household items that you want to be a bit more muted. You can take it in a different direction altogether by presoaking the shirt and upping the contrast of the folds. Also, dyeing with indigo creates a great washed-denim effect, and works well overdyed on denim shirts, jackets, and jeans.

LEVEL quick & easy

TIE METHOD knotted

DYE METHOD immersion

CURING TIME 1 hour

TOOLS + MATERIALS

Men's light gray cotton button-down shirt

Soda ash

Fiber-reactive dye

Bucket

Measuring cup

Measuring spoons

Whisk

DYE COLOR

1. TIE

Working with a dry shirt, gather it together widthwise. Tie the entire shirt in one large knot, like you would knot a rope. Leave the collar, hem, and cuffs loose on either end of the knot, adjusting them so they are fairly evenly exposed.

TIP *Depending on the thickness and length of your fabric, you will be able to make one knot or many, or you can choose to leave some areas open to solid dyeing.*

2. PREP

Mix a dye bath, following the calculations for immersion dyeing on pages 62–63. Include the soda ash in the dye bath.

3. DYE + SET

Immerse the dry shirt in the dye bath and let it soak for an hour, stirring occasionally.

4. REVEAL

After the hour is up, rinse and wash as usual.

CLASSIC STRIPED TEE

Another way to make stripes is by folding the fabric back and forth in even pleats, like an accordion or a fan, and then dyeing the edges. Folding gives a much more precise line than gathering and binding ever could. To achieve even more defined lines in this project, we will work with a thickening agent and a dry garment to cut down on the amount that the dye will bleed. Despite the precision of the folding, the application of the dye still gives the shirt the wonderful handmade feel that makes tie-dye so attractive.

LEVEL intermediate

TIE METHOD folding

DYE METHOD direct application

CURING TIME 24 hours

TOOLS + MATERIALS

- Off-white long-sleeve cotton T-shirt
- Sodium alginate
- Soda ash
- 2 squeeze bottles
- 2 colors of fiber-reactive dye
- 2 shallow containers
- Old newspapers
- Plastic bag or plastic wrap
- Measuring cup
- Measuring spoons
- Funnels
- Whisk

DYE COLORS

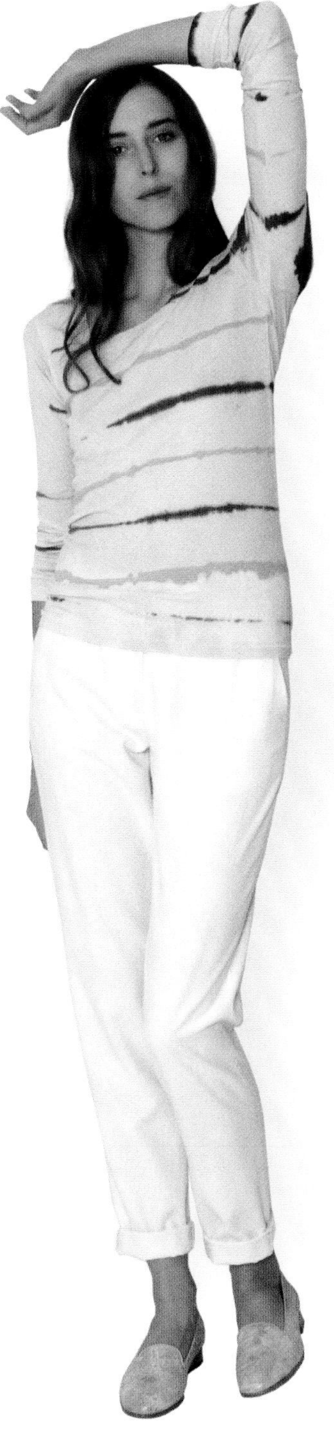

1. TIE

Working with a dry shirt, lay it flat on your workspace with the sleeves parallel to the sides. Measure 2" (5 cm) up from the hem and fold the hem up, working with both the front and back of the shirt as one. Continue to fold in horizontal pleats every 3" (7.5 cm), folding back and forth like an accordion, and making sure the edges of the pleats line up evenly. Fold the sleeves at the same intervals and position at the sides. To simplify this project, use a short-sleeved T-shirt instead.

Roll the shirt into a snail shape, carefully smoothing out wrinkles as you roll. Check that the pleats line up on both the top and bottom of the snail, and tie a rubber band loosely around the middle to secure it.

2. PREP

Prepare chemical water using soda ash, sodium alginate, and water (see page 55). You want a thick mixture for this project, so use the high end of the recommended amount of sodium alginate (I used 1 teaspoon of sodium alginate and 1 teaspoon of soda ash for 1 cup (250 ml) of water). Make enough to fill two containers with approximately 1/8"–1/4" (3–6 mm) of liquid. Each container should be wide enough to easily dip the folded T-shirt in it without touching the sides. Divide the chemical water evenly into two squeeze bottles.

After the chemical water has been thickening for about an hour, mix the first dye (see page 56) using this chemical water and pour it into the first container, being careful not to splash the edges. Repeat for the second color, pouring it into the second container.

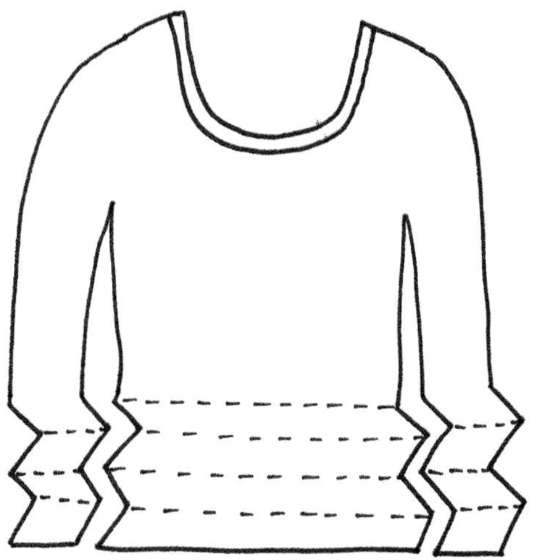

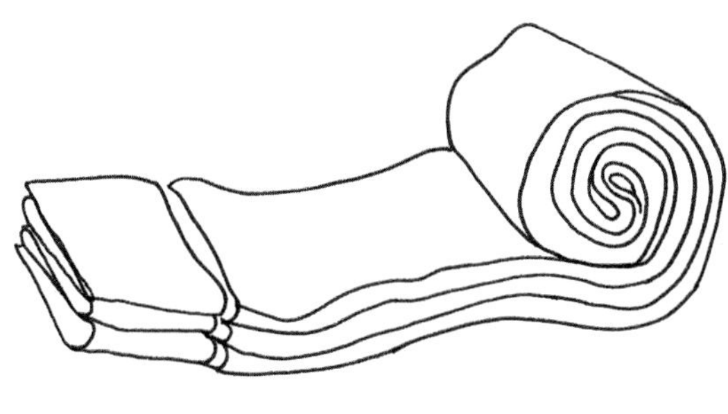

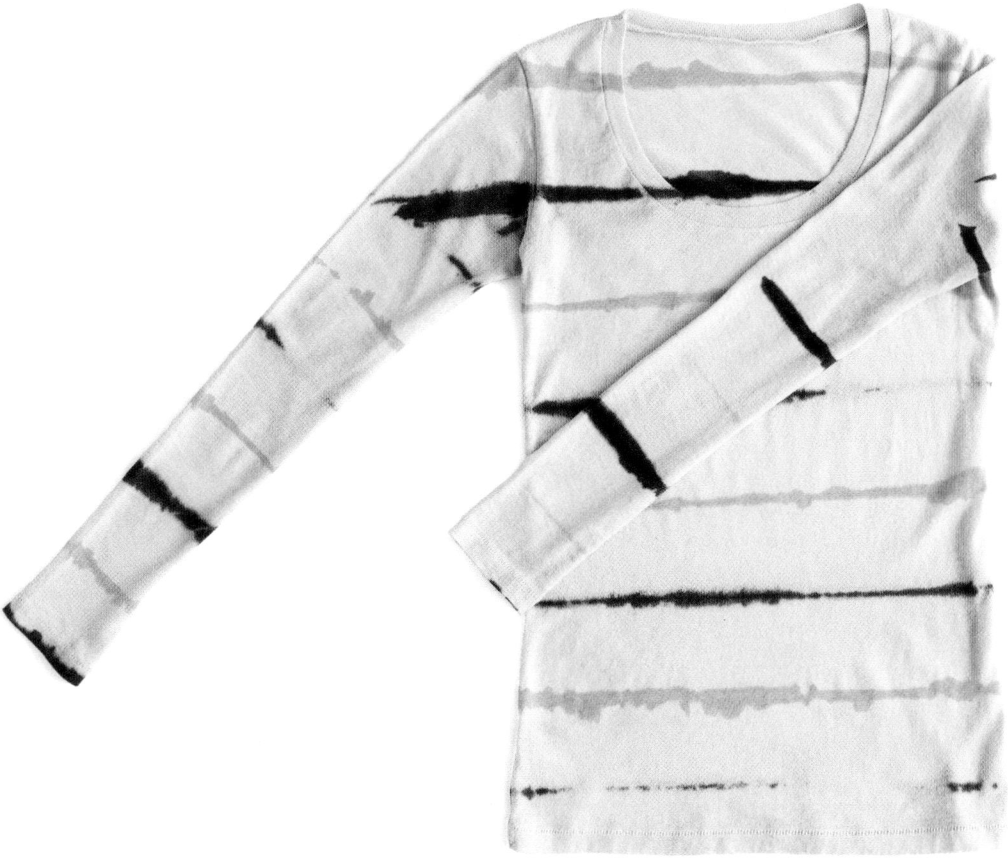

3. DYE + SET

Starting with the first color, set the snail, one spiral side down, in the dye container. Leave for about a minute, until the edge of each pleat has been saturated, then remove and dab the excess dye on some newspaper.

Let the excess dye drain out onto newspaper for about a minute, then flip the snail over and repeat the process for the second color on the opposite side.

4. CURE + REVEAL

Cover in plastic and leave for 24 hours, then rinse and wash as usual.

ALTERNATIVE *This technique can also be used to create wide stripes by dipping each edge halfway up the side of the bundle.*

TECHNIQUE: FOLDING

This is a favorite technique among my students. There's something really nice about the rigidity of the folding alongside the organic nature of the dyeing. By folding the fabric in different ways, we are able to create repeated designs such as stripes, squares, triangles, or random shapes. You can also combine large folds with other tying methods such as striping, stitching, or painting to create bold, mirrored effects or repeat designs.

Fabric can be folded randomly or perfectly even, and dyed using any method. Each technique for folding, for securing or clamping, and for dyeing will yield different results, and the combination of the three makes exponential variations possible. There are endless ways to fold fabrics for dyeing, and Japanese *shibori* can be a wonderful place to begin gathering inspiration for this method.

LATTICE TABLECLOTH

Using the same accordion-fold technique as in the previous project, you can also make a grid, which you can either dye a single color or use to create a multicolored effect as we will do in this project. In all folding projects, the more layers or the thicker the fabric, the less defined the results will be. When working with a particularly large piece of fabric, enlarge the folding pattern for sharper lines, or use a small folding pattern for thicker, hazier lines.

LEVEL advanced

TIE METHOD folding

DYE METHOD direct application

CURING TIME 24 hours

TOOLS + MATERIALS

White cotton tablecloth

Sodium alginate

Soda ash

4 squeeze bottles

4 colors of fiber-reactive dye

Old newspapers

Plastic bag or plastic wrap

Measuring cup

Measuring spoons

Funnels

Whisk

DYE COLORS

1. PREP + SET

Prepare chemical water using soda ash, sodium alginate, and water (see page 55). You want a thick mixture for this project, so use the high end of the recommended amount of sodium alginate.

After the chemical water has been thickening for about an hour, use it to mix 4 dye colors in individual squeeze bottles (see page 56). Choose colors that will overlap nicely where they meet at the corners.

2. TIE

Meanwhile, accordion-fold the dry tablecloth lengthwise in even pleats, about 8" (20.5 cm) wide. Adjust the width of the pleats based on your tablecloth to make sure the edges of the pleats line up evenly. Repeat in the opposite direction, so that you are left with a square stack of fabric. You can iron the fabric as you fold if you need a little extra help keeping the pleats in place. Your stack of fabric should have two sides opposite each other where each pleat is visible, and the other two sides will have fewer, fatter folds.

3. DYE

Place the stack on some newspaper to catch excess dye. Using your first color, apply the dye to one of the sides of the stack that has more visible pleats, making sure to dye each pleat of the fabric. Repeat on the opposite side with your second color.

Now, apply your third color to one of the sides that has fewer, fatter folds, squeezing the dye on the edge of each fold. Carefully open the fat folds, one at a time, and check to see if the dye soaked through to the inside. If it didn't, dye along the inside of the fold with the same color. Finally, repeat with your fourth color on the last remaining side.

4. CURE + REVEAL

Cover in plastic and leave for 24 hours, then rinse and wash as usual, being very careful not to let the dye redeposit on the white areas of the tablecloth.

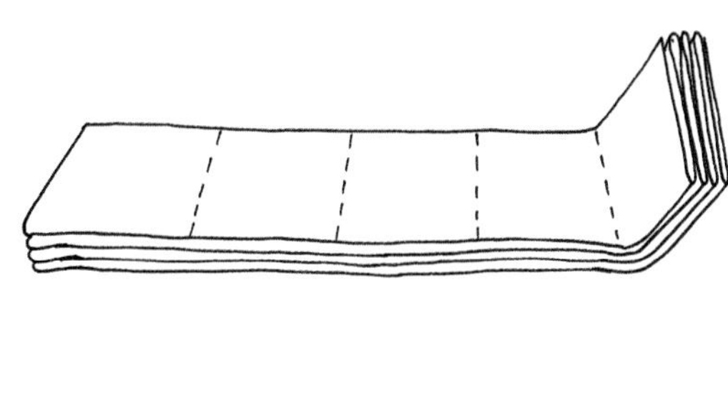

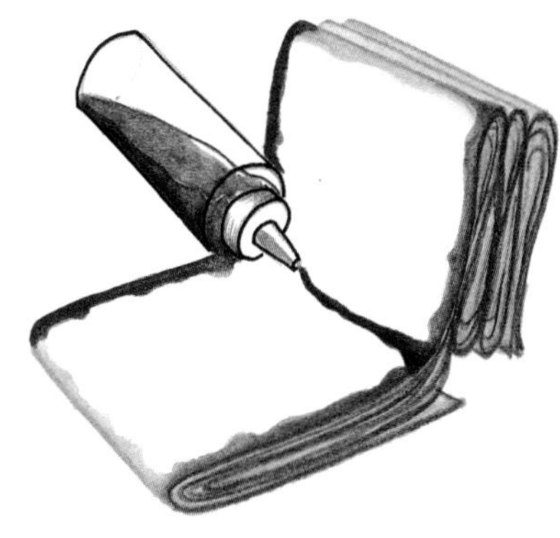

KALEIDOSCOPE BLOUSE

This is another of my favorite tying patterns, and I use it regularly with new colors or dyeing techniques for endless variation. It begins with the same accordion-folded stripe as in previous projects, but this time the stripe is then folded into a right triangle. The triangle creates a repeat pattern that offers different results depending on how you apply your dye and what colors you use. It can be beautiful in monochrome, in bright colors, or in subtle pastel hues as pictured here.

LEVEL intermediate

TIE METHOD folding

DYE METHOD direct application

CURING TIME 6 hours

TOOLS + MATERIALS

Off-white silk blouse
Soda ash
Bucket
4 colors of fiber-reactive dye
4 squeeze bottles
Old newspapers
Plastic bag or plastic wrap
Measuring cup
Measuring spoons
Funnels
Whisk

DYE COLORS

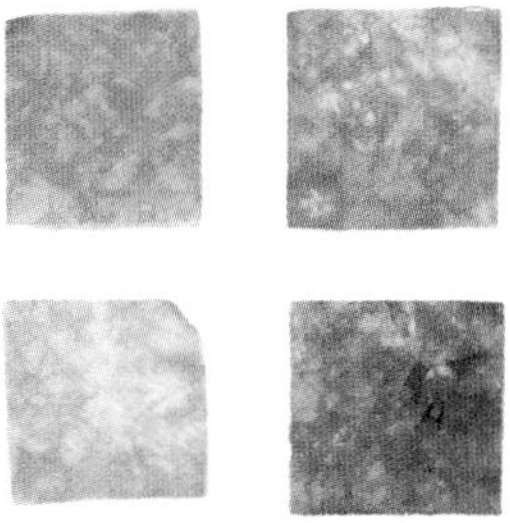

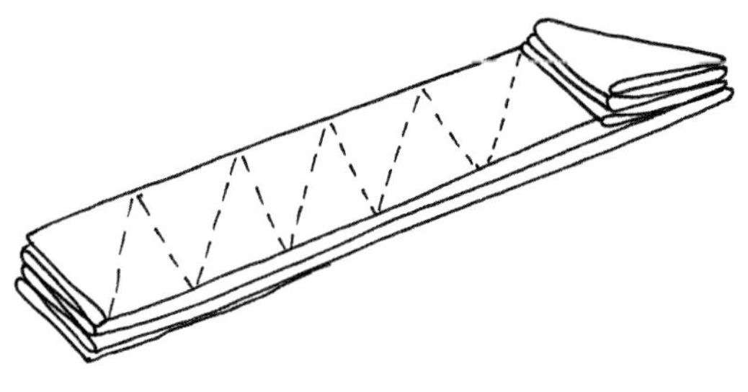

1. SET

Following the directions on page 54, presoak the blouse in soda ash for 30 minutes and wring out.

2. PREP

While the blouse is soaking, mix each color of dye in an individual squeeze bottle (see page 56).

3. TIE

Lay the blouse on a clean surface and smooth out any wrinkles. Fold in half lengthwise to find the center of the blouse, then accordion-fold the top layer into 3 sections. If the sleeve sticks out farther than the side of the blouse, accordion-fold it in last. Flip the blouse over and repeat with the bottom layer. Fold the bottom corner up at a 45-degree angle so it forms a right triangle. Repeat this process until you are left with a stack of fabric in the shape of a right triangle, making sure to accordion-fold back and forth so that all fabric is dyed evenly.

4. DYE

Place the stack on some newspaper to catch any excess dye during the dye process. Starting with one of the 45-degree corners, squeeze the first dye color onto the surface and in between the folds, just where you want that color to be. Keep in mind that the dye will bleed further out from where you put it. Repeat for the opposite corner with the second color.

Squeeze the third dye color along the diagonal edge, making sure to dye each fold of the fabric. Carefully lift the fabric layers from the opposite corner and check to see if the dye soaked through the fabric to the other side. If it didn't, dye along the inside of the diagonal with the same color.

Use the final dye color to dye the remaining undyed areas of the fabric. Repeat the lifting process and carefully dye the inside of the stack of fabric so the dye is evenly distributed throughout the entire blouse.

5. CURE + REVEAL

Loosely cover the stack in plastic wrap or carefully place it inside a plastic bag. Make sure the dyes aren't dripping; you don't want the color from one area to muddy up another. Leave for 6 hours and then rinse and wash as usual.

SHIBORI NAPKINS

With the same folding technique and the same dye color, subtle differences in the application of the dye can produce myriad results. In this project, we will fold each of the napkins into identical perfect triangles, and then use boards and clamps positioned in different ways to create a unique relief effect on each. Even a subtle shift in where the board is placed will make a large impact on the design once the fabric is unfolded and the repeat becomes visible. These make a wonderful set of napkins—they're visually cohesive, but each guest at your dinner party gets a unique design!

LEVEL advanced

TIE METHOD folding

DYE METHOD immersion

CURING TIME 1 hour

TOOLS + MATERIALS

Set of white cotton napkins

Soda ash

2 buckets, one large enough to fit fabric with clamps

Fiber-reactive dye

Pairs of boards to clamp onto fabric, in a variety of shapes

Clamps and rubber bands

Measuring cup

Measuring spoons

Whisk

DYE COLOR

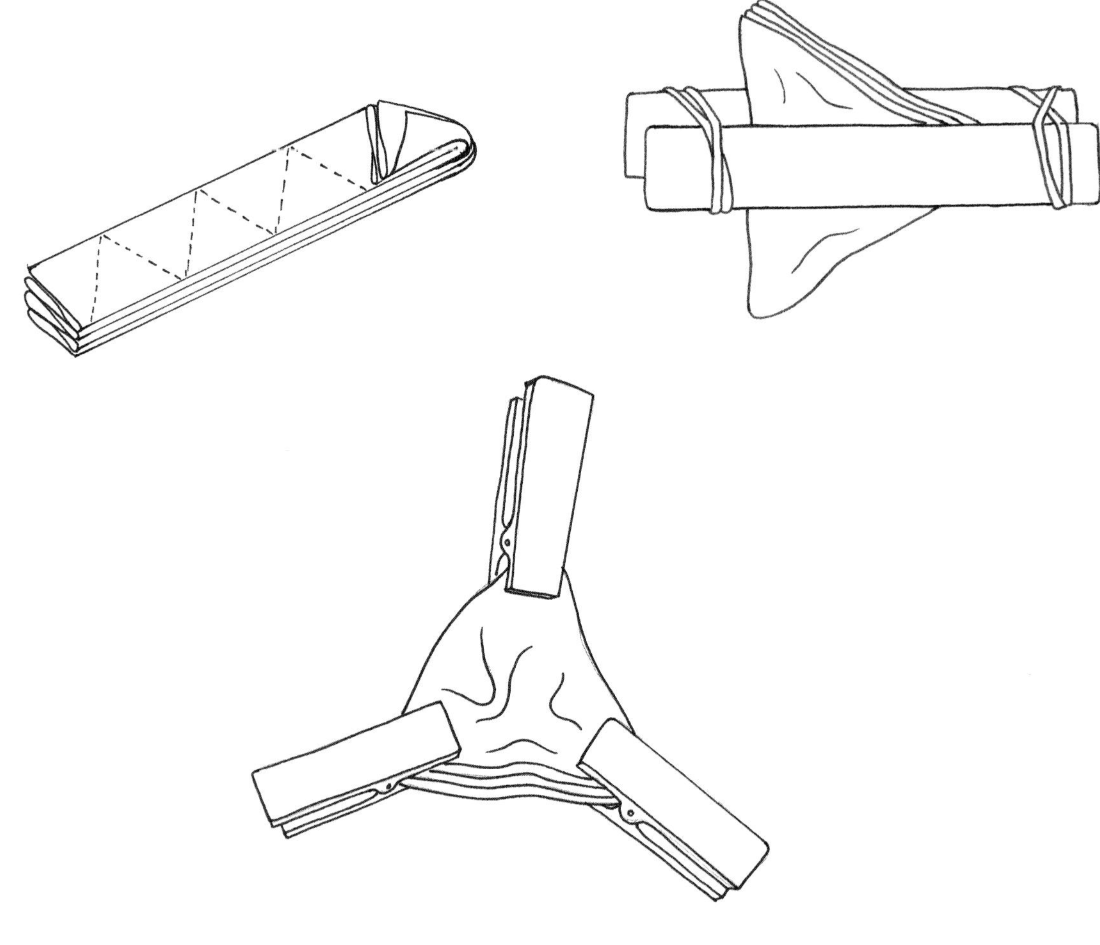

1. SET

Following the directions on page 54, presoak the napkins in soda ash for 30 minutes and wring out.

2. PREP

While the napkins are presoaking, mix a dye bath. Use the calculations for immersion dyeing (pages 62–63), skipping the soda ash since you are already presoaking.

3. TIE

Starting with the first napkin, accordion-fold lengthwise into 6 sections. Fold the bottom corner up at a 30-degree angle. Flip the fabric over and fold the diagonal edge to meet the side of the fabric strip, forming a perfect equilateral triangle. Repeat this process until you are left with a stack of fabric in the shape of an equilateral triangle, making sure to accordion-fold back and forth so that all fabric is dyed evenly. Repeat with each napkin.

Starting with the first napkin, sandwich it between two matching boards. Check that the boards are lined up, and then clamp them

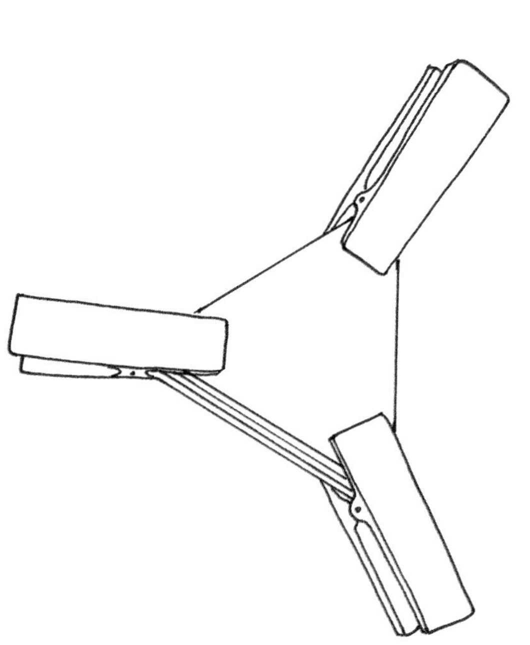

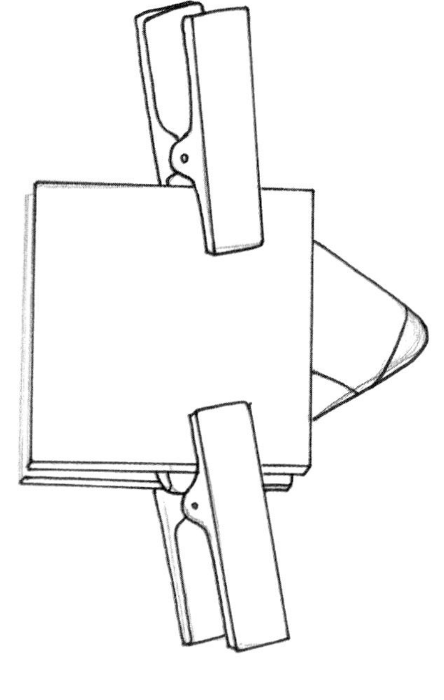

tightly around the napkin. Feel free to improvise with your boards and clamps; you can use any rigid plastic or wooden items as boards, and hold them in place with C-clamps, binder clips, clothespins, spring clamps, or rubber bands. Repeat with various board shapes on each of the napkins. Each shape will create a different pattern. The same shape, placed in a different position on the triangle, can also create surprisingly different designs.

TIP: *To achieve a symmetrical design centered on a square napkin, fold the fabric like the paper fortune-teller you used to make in elementary school.*

---

4. DYE

Immerse the napkins in the dye bath and let them soak for an hour.

---

5. REVEAL

After the hour is up, rinse and wash as usual.

MOUNTAIN PEAKS TEE

Folds don't have to be rigid. Think about folding more randomly, folding the fabric in on itself instead of like an accordion, or folding individual areas of your fabric differently. In this project, we will create the subtlest, softest folds simply by pulling the fabric up into loose peaks. We will then create a shadow of the folds by spraying the dye mixture lightly onto the fabric so that when it is unfolded later, an echo of the peaks is left behind.

LEVEL quick & easy

TIE METHOD folding

DYE METHOD direct application

CURING TIME 24 hours

TOOLS + MATERIALS

Gray cotton T-shirt

Fiber-reactive dye in a color slightly darker than the shirt

Soda ash

Spray bottle

Old newspapers

Plastic tarp

Measuring cup

Measuring spoons

Funnel

Whisk

DYE COLOR

1. PREP

Mix the dye in a spray bottle, including soda ash since you aren't presoaking (see page 56). Use 1 teaspoon of soda ash for 1 cup (250 ml) of dye.

2. TIE

Lay a dry T-shirt on a clean work surface with the front facing up. Place plastic or newspaper inside the shirt to protect the back while you dye the front. Pull the fabric of the shirt up into loose, random peaks. Position the main front body of the T-shirt this way and leave the hem, neck, arms, and back flat on the table.

3. DYE

Spray the dye onto the peaks, spraying toward the center of the shirt and avoiding the outer areas. Spray from one general direction, so that the area behind the fabric peaks remains undyed.

4. CURE + REVEAL

Cover loosely in plastic. Leave for 24 hours, then rinse and wash as usual, being careful not to let the dye redeposit on the undyed areas of the shirt.

TRITIK SCARF

To create a repeat pattern, fold the fabric before stitching it. Thinner fabric and fewer folds will create a clearer repeat. To enhance the image even more, stitch two parallel rows of thread closely together to get a thicker line. Any design can be stitched onto the folded fabric, but the repeat often looks best using simple geometric shapes.

LEVEL advanced

TIE METHOD folding & stitching

DYE METHOD immersion

CURING TIME 1 hour

TOOLS + MATERIALS

White rectangular cotton scarf

Chalk or water-soluble marker

Needle

Strong thread (undyed or polyester so the thread color doesn't bleed)

Fiber-reactive dye

Salt

Bucket

Soda ash

Measuring cup and spoons

Whisk

DYE COLOR

ALTERNATIVE *I wanted this scarf to be a true, strong black, which can often be hard to achieve. In order to do so, I used the standard immersion dye method and added salt, but you can use any immersion method on page 66 and skip the salt if you decide on a different color.*

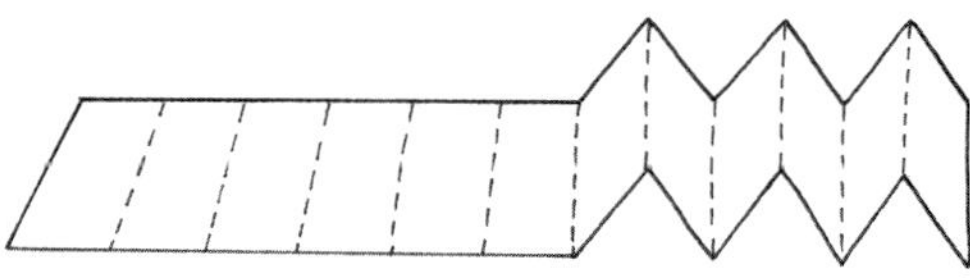

1. TIE

Measure the width of your scarf, divide in half, and make a note of this measurement. Lay the scarf flat on your work space. Starting at the center of the scarf, make a mark at every interval of your number, out to each end. Using these marks as guides, accordion-fold the scarf, making sure the edges of the folds line up evenly. You will be left with a rectangular stack of fabric. Fold this rectangle in half to create a square stack and smooth out any wrinkles.

Mark your design with chalk or a water-soluble marker, imagining the design mirroring at the folds. For my design, I created a quarter circle around the center fold on the corner furthest from the hem, so that when opened it forms a complete circle. About 2" (5 cm) away, I created a diagonal line framing the opposite corner.

Choose a sturdy, thick thread, or double it for strength, as you will be working with an entire stack of fabric. Thread the needle and tie a knot in one end. Sew a running stitch along your design, sewing all the way through the stack of fabric, and leaving enough thread at either end to grab on to. The thicker your fabric is, or the more layers you have, the wider your stitches should be.

Pull the thread from both ends, gathering the fabric tightly around it until it is fully compressed. Wetting the fabric before pulling the thread may make it easier to gather. Tie the thread in a sturdy knot to hold the gathers in place.

2. PREP

Mix the dye bath, using the standard immersion dye method (pages 62–63) to achieve even coverage on untied areas. Dissolve the salt in a bit of hot water to add to the bath before immersing the scarf, and mix the soda ash mixture separately, setting it aside to add later. Make sure that all of the water in your different mixtures equals the total amount that you need.

3. DYE

Wet the scarf in plain water so that it is fully and evenly saturated, then wring out. Immerse it in the dye bath and stir for 15 minutes to ensure even coverage.

4. SET

After 15 minutes, lift the scarf out of the bucket and add the soda ash mixture to the dye bath. Stir well, then place the scarf back in the bath. Let soak for an hour, stirring occasionally.

5. REVEAL

After the hour is up, rinse, then clip the threads and pull them out, revealing your design. Wash as usual.

TECHNIQUE: STITCHING

Another age-old technique for dyeing fabric is stitch-resist. Often referred to by the Javanese term *tritik* or the Yoruban term *adire alabere*, designs are stitched into the fabric and pulled tightly before dyeing. Each stitch leaves behind a small, undyed mark, so that the memory of the stitching is clearly visible within the design.

Stitch-resist can be used as a tool to shade or to create shapes. Basic shapes and images also benefit from this technique, since it allows for a specific area to be blocked off and dyed a separate color, as seen in the beautiful simplicity of some abstract Indonesian tapestries, and also in the pictorial hippie T-shirts displaying peace signs and hearts. Overall gathered effects reminiscent of the scrunch or stripe methods are created by sewing entire areas with parallel running stitches. Because this process is so time consuming, fabric is often folded first and sewn in layers, and the folding is frequently utilized to create complex repeat designs. Stitching allows for control over the image in a way that other techniques don't; any image envisioned can be created: geometric, pictorial, or organic.

STARFISH ROMPER

The easiest way to make an iconic, or easily recognizable image is to stitch just the outline, creating a simple silhouette. You can dye the garment one color, or easily separate different sections on either side of your stitching to remain undyed or done in a different color. The nature of stitch-resist is a feathered effect around where the thread gathers the fabric together. If you want to get the freehand design possibilities of stitch-resist with less feathering, you can pull your thread tight and then wrap a rubber band around the fabric where it gathers to get a sharper line.

LEVEL intermediate

TIE METHOD stitching

DYE METHOD immersion

CURING TIME 1 hour

TOOLS + MATERIALS

White cotton baby romper

Chalk or water-soluble marker

Needle

Strong thread (undyed or polyester so the thread color doesn't bleed)

Plastic bag

Rubber band

Soda ash

Fiber-reactive dye

Salt

2 buckets

Measuring cup

Measuring spoons

Whisk

DYE COLOR

1. TIE

Select a design. Sketch the outline on the romper with fabric chalk or a water-soluble marker. If you want a little extra help, print out a template to scale from the Internet, cut it out, and trace around it. Skip this step if you want to freehand the design.

Choose a sturdy, thick thread, or double sewing thread for strength. Thread the needle and tie a knot in one end. Stitch along the outline of the design using a running stitch, sewing only through the front layer of the romper.

Pull the thread, gathering the fabric tightly until it is fully compressed. Wetting the fabric before pulling the thread may make it easier to gather. Tie the thread in a sturdy knot to hold the gathers in place.

2. PREP, DYE, SET

Follow steps 2 through 5 on page 136 to prep, dye, and finish the romper.

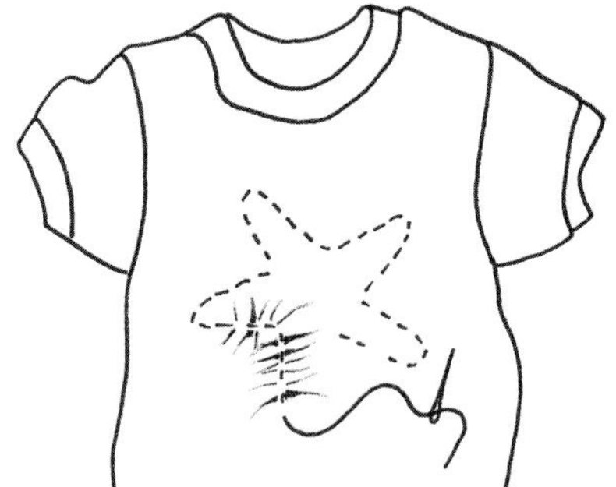

ALTERNATIVE: *Try wrapping the interior in plastic as you did with the polka dot dress on page 92. This will give you a solid design as pictured in the romper on the left.*

WATERCOLOR DRESS

I'm not a great painter, but you would never know it by looking at this dress! Although you can paint on any fabric, silk takes the dye so well, and the colors blend so smoothly, that anyone can do it and look like a pro. Take advantage of the wrinkles of the fabric, air bubbles, and any irregularities of your work surface to create textural effects in your design. Alternatively, to get a smoother look, stretch the fabric and paint on it while it is suspended in the air.

LEVEL quick & easy

TIE METHOD untied

DYE METHOD direct application

CURING TIME 6 hours

TOOLS + MATERIALS

- Off-white silk dress
- Soda ash
- Bucket
- 3-5 colors of fiber-reactive dye
- 3-5 squeeze bottles
- 3-5 small containers (I like to reuse single serving yogurt containers for this)
- Paintbrushes
- Plastic tarp
- Measuring cup
- Measuring spoons
- Funnels
- Whisk

DYE COLORS

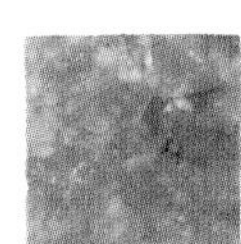

1. SET

Following the directions on page 54, presoak the dress in soda ash for 30 minutes and wring out.

2. PREP

While the dress is soaking, mix each dye color in an individual squeeze bottle (see page 56). Pour some of each color into separate small containers for painting, reserving the rest. Refill your containers as necessary during the painting process. The leftovers in the bottles can be saved for later dye projects, but any dyes remaining in the paint containers should be discarded as they will be contaminated by soda ash from your paintbrushes.

3. DYE

Lay the dress flat on a plastic tarp and paint on it as you would on canvas. For this dress, I watered down my full-strength dyes to create pastels and different tints of the same colors. Because the fabric is wet, colors will bleed and run beautifully like watercolor. Dye will bleed more on a smooth fabric like silk charmeuse, and less on an absorbent fabric like cotton jersey. The dye will also bleed through thin fabrics, including most silks, so there is no need to turn the dress over and paint the other side, which could be messy. It's best to paint from the front and leave the dress flat to cure.

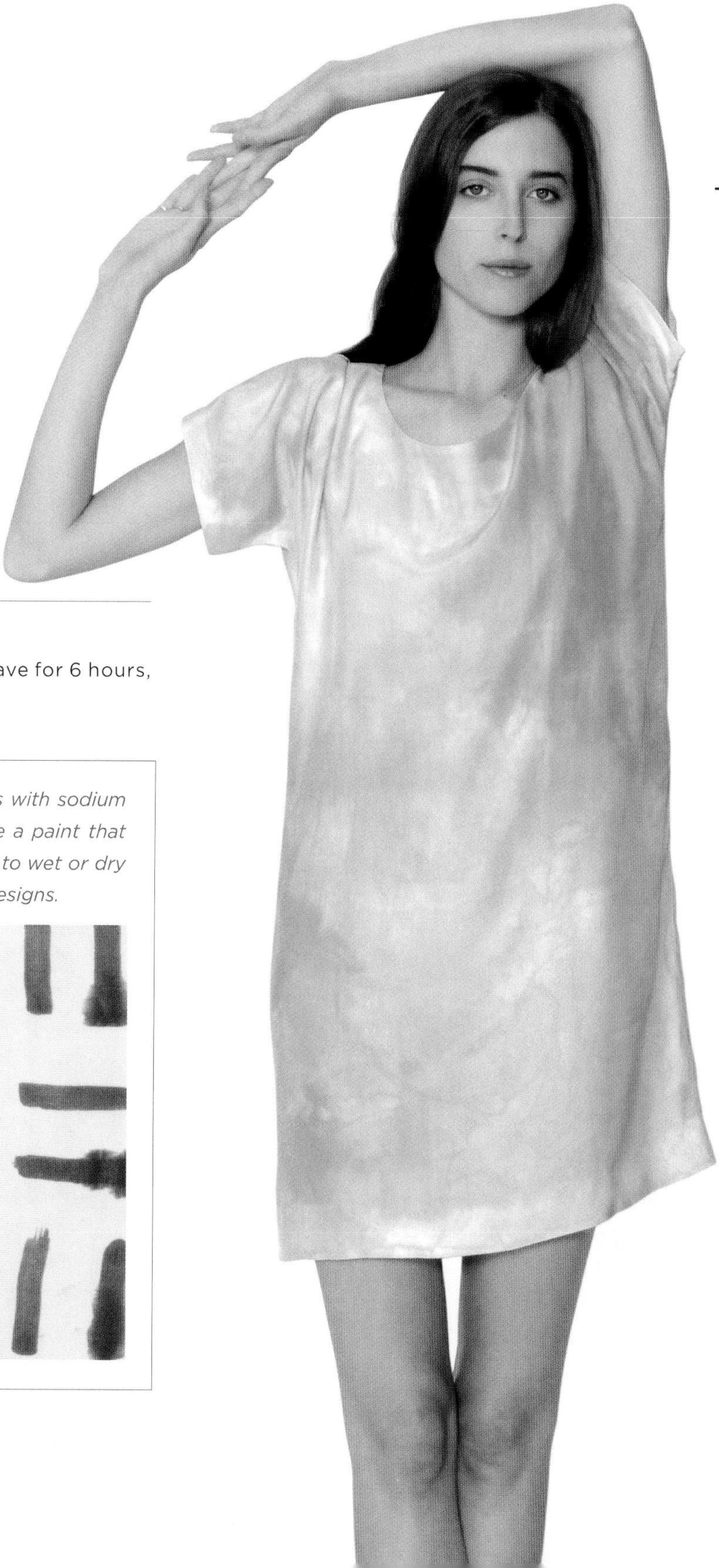

4. CURE + REVEAL

Cover loosely with plastic and leave for 6 hours, then rinse and wash as usual.

ALTERNATIVE: *Thicken the dyes with sodium alginate (see page 55) to create a paint that spreads less and can be applied to wet or dry fabric for use in more detailed designs.*

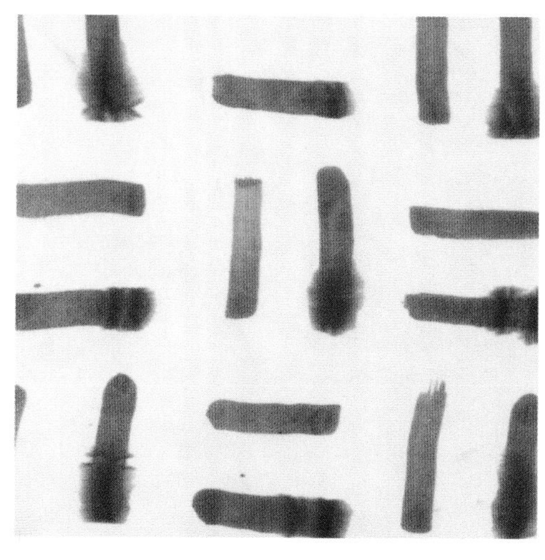

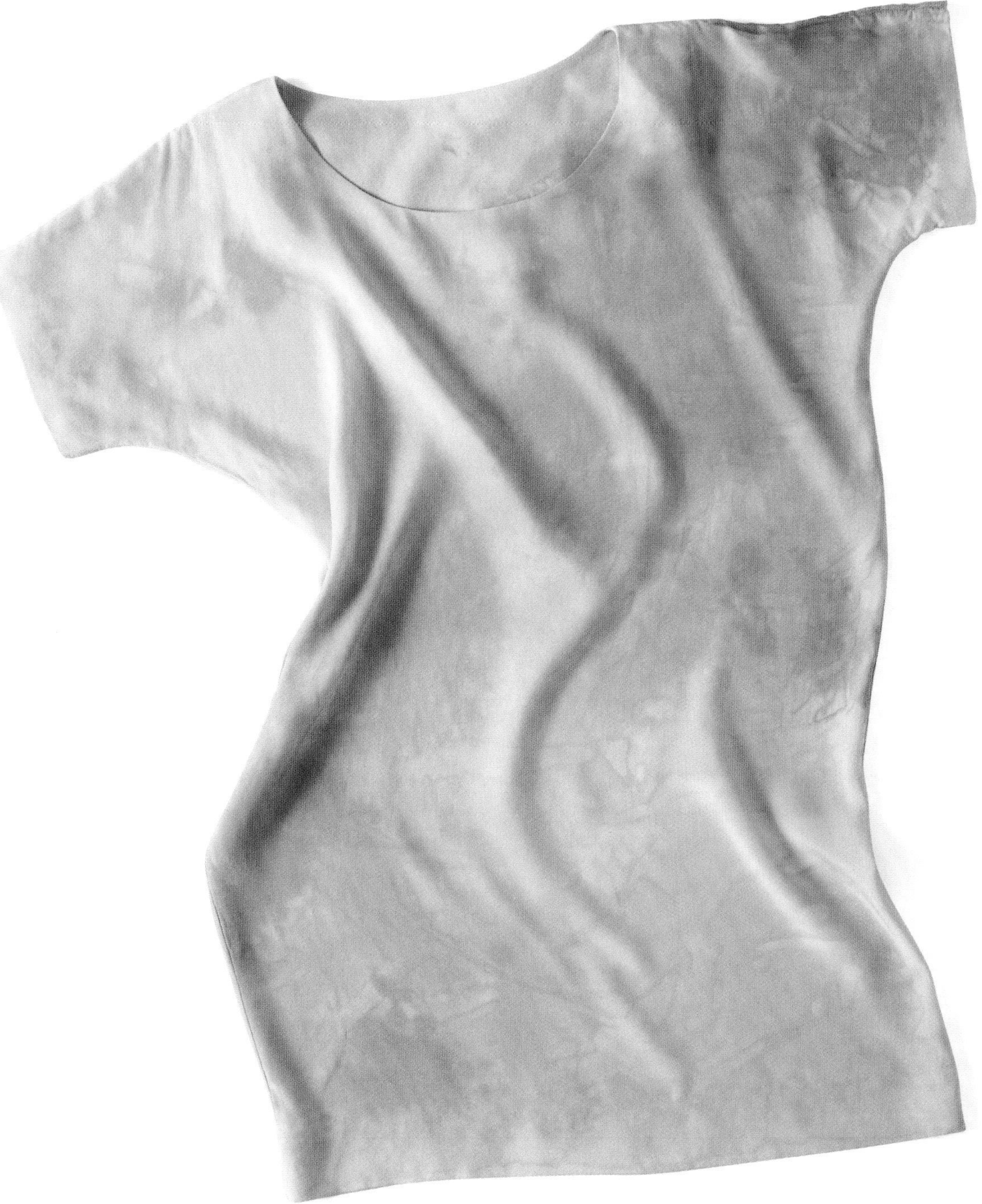

TIP *Try sprinkling rock salt on the dress as you apply the dye. The salt will attract the moisture and create interesting patterns. This works especially well when the garment is stretched and suspended.*

TECHNIQUE: UNTIED METHODS

Using the same dyes and many of the same tools, you can open up a world of possibilities by simply leaving your fabric untied. Treating fabric as a canvas, you can use dyes as paints by adding water or a thickening additive; you can flick, squirt, spray, or splatter the dye; or simply dip your garment in a bath to create an ombré effect. You can also use this method in conjunction with other techniques; for example, try folding your fabric before painting to create a repeat design. Dyeing with untied methods allows you to work with accessories and objects that you wouldn't be able to bind or tie, such as sneakers or lampshades.

DIP-DYE TOTE

True ombré is surprisingly difficult to achieve, but this simple dip-dye version allows you to create the same effect without all of the hassle. Try dyeing it dry for a more distinct line, as pictured below, or wetting it first so that the dye wicks up and creates more of a gradient, as pictured on the opposite page. You could also try dipping it in more than one dye bath, submerging one color further than the other for another variation.

LEVEL beginner

TIE METHOD untied

DYE METHOD immersion

CURING TIME 1 hour

TOOLS + MATERIALS

- Unbleached canvas tote
- Skirt hanger with clips
- Fiber-reactive dye
- Soda ash
- Bucket
- Measuring cup
- Measuring spoons
- Whisk

DYE COLOR

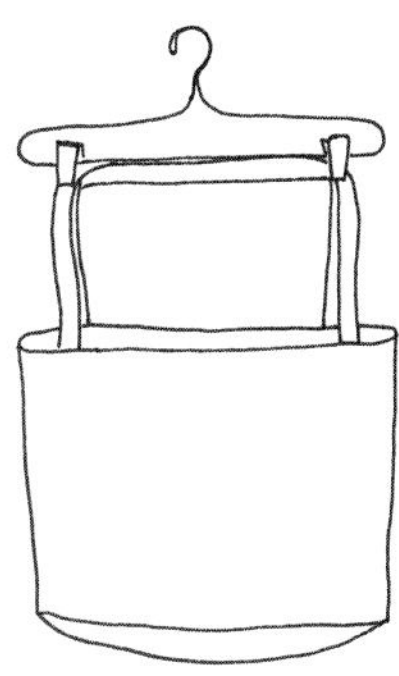

1. PREP

Choose a bucket wide enough to fit the tote bag without folding or gathering. Smooth out any wrinkles and clip it onto a skirt hanger. Find a place to hang it so that the bottom will fall just above the base of your bucket. Set it aside while you mix your dye bath. Mix the dye bath, following the calculations for immersion dyeing on pages 62–63. Include the soda ash in the dye bath.

2. DYE + SET

Dip the tote into the dye bath, stopping just below where you want the dye to end, since it may bleed and wick up further. Make sure to lower the tote evenly so the dye line is straight. Let it soak in the dye bath for 1 hour without stirring.

3. REVEAL

After the hour is up, carefully lift it out of your dye bath and transfer it to a sink, making sure not to get dye above the dye line. To keep the undyed areas clean, rinse and hand wash the tote with the dyed part toward the bottom so the excess dye runs straight into the sink. Hang to dry in the same direction.

OMBRÉ DAY GOWN

A perfect ombré gradient may take a little time and patience, but the results can be worth the effort. The smooth transition of color is probably one of the most stunning and simple hand-dyed effects. Use calsolene oil to break the surface tension and allow for a smoother gradient. Raising the garment slowly and continuously over the course of the dye bath will also help to ensure a smooth gradient. I achieved the multiple colors in this garment by chance; I used gray dye on silk and the color changed hue toward the bottom of the skirt as it was immersed in the dye bath for a longer period of time. If you like this multicolored effect, you can also achieve it by dipping your garment in more than one dye bath.

LEVEL advanced

TIE METHOD untied

DYE METHOD immersion

CURING TIME 1 hour

TOOLS + MATERIALS

- Off-white long silk dress
- Skirt hanger with clips
- String
- Soda ash
- 2 buckets
- Fiber-reactive dye
- Salt
- Calsolene oil
- Measuring cup
- Measuring spoons
- Whisk

DYE COLOR

1. SET & PREP

Choose a bucket wide enough to fit the skirt of the dress without folding or gathering. Find a place to hang it so that the bottom will fall just above the base of your bucket, and a way to continually raise it to create the ombré effect. I attached my hanger to string and looped it over a shower rod to help me raise it smoothly.

Following the directions on page 54, presoak the dress in soda ash in a separate bucket for 30 minutes and wring out.

While the dress is presoaking, mix a dye bath including salt and calsolene oil, following the calculations for immersion dyeing on pages 62–63, and additives on page 55. Include soda ash in the dye bath as well; this project works better when you double up on the soda ash.

2. DYE

After you wring out your dress, smooth out any wrinkles and clip it onto a skirt hanger. Since I dyed a long dress, I secured it at the waist, which also allowed me to ensure the skirt was unwrinkled; if you do the same, make sure to keep the top of the dress away from the dye bath.

Dip the skirt of the dress into the dye bath, stopping just below where you want the top of your gradient to be, since it may bleed and wick up further. Make sure the fabric falls even and straight.

Slowly and continuously raise the skirt out of the dye bath over the course of an hour. The smoother and more consistently you raise it, the less likely it will be that you will have any sharp lines in your end results. If you reach the bottom and parts of it aren't as dark as you'd like, you can lower and raise again.

TIP *Dyeing for an hour is best, but it can be hard to raise and lower the dress for that long, so if you're happy with your results after a half hour or 45 minutes go ahead and wash it out, just know that it might wash out lighter.*

3. REVEAL

After you've finished dyeing your dress, carefully lift it out of the dye bath and transfer it to a sink or shower, making sure not to get dye above the dye line. To keep the undyed areas clean, rinse and hand wash the dress with the dyed part toward the bottom so the excess dye runs straight down the drain. Hang to dry in the same direction.

PROBLEM SOLVING

CAN I TIE-DYE WITH OTHER TYPES OF DYE?

In this book I teach you to use fiber-reactive dyes because they are the easiest, safest, and most versatile, but you are welcome to use any dyes that you like or have on hand. Keep in mind that any dyes that need to be boiled or used in a washing machine lend themselves best to the immersion dyeing methods, which tend to be monochromatic.

ARE NATURAL DYES SAFER THAN SYNTHETIC DYES?

Natural doesn't necessarily translate to safe. Most natural dyes are, but the mordants needed to bond the color to the fabric, like metals and, surprisingly, rhubarb leaves, can sometimes be more toxic and harsh on the environment. Fiber-reactive dyes and soda ash, on the other hand, are safer than most household cleaning products. See the chart on page 152 for more information.

CAN I TIE-DYE IN A WASHING MACHINE?

Yes, you can use fiber-reactive dyes or any other type of dye made for the machine. This will only work for single colored tie-dye like the immersion bath methods, not for the multicolored effect you get with direct applications.

DOES THE TEMPERATURE OF THE WATER AFFECT THE VIBRANCY OF THE COLORS?

Fiber-reactive dyes are formulated to be used with room temperature water, so hot water will cause them to begin to activate immediately, bonding the dye to the water before it has a chance to bond with your fabric, resulting in less vibrant colors. Cold water, on the other hand, requires a longer curing process.

THE COLORS DIDN'T COME OUT THE WAY THEY LOOKED ON THE BOTTLE OR IN THE BOOK.

There are so many variables that it is close to impossible to copy or replicate a specific color. The same dye will come out different based on many factors (see page 65). If you want to get a specific color, run tests first with the fabric you plan on dyeing, but otherwise embrace the unpredictability of dyeing!

I GOT THE WRONG COLOR DYE ON MY PROJECT, CAN I FIX IT WHILE I'M WORKING?

You can try to water it down immediately or go over it with another color so it becomes diluted. If that doesn't work it might be time to improvise and change the color of your garment!

WILL THERE BE A PROBLEM IF I DON'T LET THE FABRIC CURE AS LONG AS RECOMMENDED?

The colors may come out lighter, but even with the 5 minutes of curing that I do during demos in dye class, the color still bonds. They may also be less permanent, and fade over time.

WHAT IF I LEAVE IT FOR LONGER?

Leaving your garment curing longer won't hurt it, but after about 24 hours you won't see any change in color—so it doesn't help either. Feel free to leave it longer if it fits your schedule.

THE FABRIC DIDN'T TAKE THE DYE, OR THE COLOR SEEMS TO BE FADING AND WASHING OUT OF MY CLOTHES. WHY ISN'T IT PERMANENT?

Did you remember to use soda ash? Were you using expired or old dye? Did you let your garment cure for long enough? Did you keep it wet while curing? Are you using natural fibers? All of these will have an effect on the penetration and permanence of the dye.

WHY DIDN'T MY THREAD DYE?

Most store-bought clothes are sewn with polyester thread because it's stronger, but polyester doesn't take fiber-reactive dyes. If you don't like how that looks, try to buy clothes to dye that don't have a lot of visible topstitching. If you make your own clothes use cotton thread or dye the fabric first. Also, most PFD (prepared for dyeing) clothes come sewn with cotton thread. (Dharma Trading online carries a great assortment. See page 156 for more details.)

THERE IS TOO MUCH WHITE IN MY DESIGN.

This is one of the most common problems for beginners who are often timid about applying too much dye. When bottle dyeing, make sure to get the nozzle inside the folds, and then check that you saturated the garment throughout. For immersion dyeing, try tying more loosely; also, using the all-in-one or standard bath methods (page 66) will allow the dyes to penetrate further than if it is presoaked.

THE COLORS TURNED OUT ALL MUDDY.

Another common problem for beginners, If you are applying too much dye or too many colors, and especially if you are overlapping colors that become brown when mixed, you will get muddy results. Complementary colors (page 44) generally create a muddy brown, so avoid those if you want clearer tones. And don't overload your washing machine during the rinsing out process.

I HAVE EXPLOSIONS OF UNMIXED DYE ALL OVER MY PROJECT. HOW CAN I AVOID IT?

Some dyes are harder to mix than others; I often have explosions of fuchsia appearing in unexpected colors like gray and black. Mixing dye with urea (see page 55) will help dissolve all of the stubborn dye powder. If you're really having trouble you can filter the dye through a fine strainer. Finally, be sure to work on a clean surface, as even tiny specks of dye powder can cause big trouble.

WHY DID I GET STAINING ON MY UNDYED AREAS?

Make sure to rinse and wash your garment properly (page 59), and don't leave it in a wet ball afterward. Even when it seems like the excess dye is all gone you will need to machine-wash and dry it once before the color truly sets. If you don't have a washing machine, just hang it up to dry and do your final wash the next time you go to the laundromat.

MY HANDS ARE BLUE!

If you aren't wearing gloves, this can happen. Don't worry, while you don't want to make it a regular habit, the dye will wear off in a couple of days. You can also buy a specialized exfoliant called Reduran hand cleaner to help speed up the process (page 27).

UGH, I HATE MY RESULTS

I doubt many of you will feel this way. I'm almost always thrilled when I reveal a dye project, even when it went totally wrong and unexpected. One of the great things about tie-dye is if you don't like it, you can dye it again. And again, and again. And if you still don't like it you can bleach it and start all over!

CHEAT SHEET

Copy this cheat sheet to use with dirty tie-dye hands or take along to group tie-dye parties.

DIRECT APPLICATION DYEING

Each brand will provide instructions for its own dyes, but you can use this chart as a general guide.

TIP *If you want to mix soda ash directly in with the bottled dyes, add 1 teaspoon of soda ash per 1 cup (250 ml) of water. The dye will become exhausted within 24 hours.*

MIXING THE DYES

H_2O	Dye Powder	# Adult T-Shirts
½ cup (125 ml)	1 tsp	1
1 cup (250 ml)	2 tsp	2
2 cups (500 ml)	4 tsp	4
1 quart (1 l)	8 tsp	8

OPTIONAL ADDITIVES

	How to Mix	What It Does
Urea	1 tbsp per 1 cup (250 ml) warm H_2O; let cool	Helps dissolve dye, keeps fabric wet
Sodium Alginate	⅛–1 tsp per 1 cup (250 ml) H_2O; wait 1 hour	Thickens dye
Casolene Oil	½ tsp per 1 gal (4 l) H_2O	Breaks surface tension

STEPS

1. Prewash fabric.
2. Set up space.
3. Presoak fabric: Mix soda ash with water in a ratio of 1 cup to 1 gallon. Presoak fabric for ½ hour and wring out.
4. (Optional) Mix chemical solution using optional additives.
5. Mix dyes (using chemical solution or plain tap water).
6. Tie.
7. Dye with squeeze bottles, paintbrushes, or other direct application methods.
8. Cure: Cover in plastic and keep wet for 6 to 24 hours.
9. Rinse and reveal.
10. Cleanup.

IMMERSION DYEING

Each brand will provide instructions for its own dyes, but you can use this chart as a general guide.

TIP *If you already have a bottle mixed of the concentrated dye used for direct application, you can use this instead of dye powder. Use about 1/2 cup (125 ml) per gallon (4 l) of water.*

MIXING THE DYE BATH

FABRIC BY WEIGHT	APPROX. # OF T-SHIRTS	H_2O	SODA ASH	SALT (optional, or use less)	DYE POWDER (extra light)	DYE POWDER (light)	DYE POWDER (medium)	DYE POWDER (dark)	DYE POWDER (extra dark)
1½ oz (38 gms)	Baby tee	1 qt (1 l)	1½ tsp	¼ cup	⅛ tsp	¼ tsp	½ tsp	1 tsp	2 tsp
3 oz (75 gms)	1	2 qts (2 l)	1 tbsp	½ cup (125 ml)	½ tsp	¼ tsp	1 tsp	2 tsp	4 tsp
6 oz (150 gms)	2-3	1 gal (4 l)	2 tbsp	1 cup (250 ml)	½ tsp	1 tsp	2 tsp	4 tsp	8 tsp
1 lb (450 gms)	6-9	3 gal (12 l)	⅓ cup	3 cups (750 ml)	1½ tsp	1 tbsp	2 tbsp	¼ cup	½ cup (125 ml)

STEPS (STANDARD METHOD)

1. Prewash fabric.
2. Set up space.
3. Tie.
4. Mix dye bath.
5. Immerse fabric in the dye bath and stir for 15 minutes.
6. Lift fabric out of the bath, add soda ash mixture, and place fabric back in.
7. Leave to soak an additional 1 hour.
8. Rinse and reveal.
9. Cleanup.

FOR PRESOAK METHOD *Soak fabric in soda ash for 30 minutes before dyeing, then skip step 6.*

FOR ALL-IN-ONE METHOD *Mix soda ash directly into dye bath, then skip step 6.*

LIQUID MEASUREMENTS CONVERSION CHART

1 gal	4 qts	16 cups	128 oz	4 liters (approx.)
	1 qt	4 cups	32 oz	1 liter (approx.)
		1 cup	8 oz	250 ml (approx.)
			1 oz	30 ml (approx.)

DRY MEASUREMENTS CONVERSION CHART

1 cup	16 tbsp	48 tsp	250 ml (approx.)
	1 tbsp	3 tsp	15 ml (approx.)
		1 tsp	5 ml (approx.)

DIFFERENT TYPES OF DYE

	FIBER-REACTIVE	NATURAL
GENERAL INFORMATION	Fiber-reactive dyes are hands down the best, most versatile dyes for natural fibers, especially cellulose. They are bright, easy to use with multiple methods, colorfast, and nontoxic. They are also the best dye to use for multicolored dye projects. Some brands (e.g., Tulip One-Step and Jacquard iDyes) now sell the dyes premixed with the soda ash, and while they are easier to use, the dyes may be less versatile and the results less vivid.	Natural dyes are best for personal use. The process is romantic and exciting, but not good for mass production or consistency. It can be demanding and difficult, with different mordants required for different dyes; this can be both frustrating and rewarding for the hobbyist or artist who likes a challenge.
LEVEL	Easy	Difficult
FABRIC	All natural fibers; formulated for plant fibers but works on silk and wool as well	All natural fibers, especially wool
PERMANENCY	The most permanent dye available, it actually forms a molecular bond with fibers.	Not permanent; will fade over time
METHOD	Cold-water methods: direct application (single or multiple colors), immersion dye, batik, silkscreening, fabric painting	Hot-water method: immersion dye in boiling water
SAFETY: See general safety guidelines on page 20 and refer to all manufacturer's guidelines when using any dyes or chemicals.	Though nontoxic, soda ash can be a skin irritant; wear gloves.	Most dyes are safe but many mordants can be harmful or even highly toxic; "natural" does not equal safe or nontoxic.

VAT	ACID	ALL-PURPOSE	DISCHARGE DYES/ BLEACH
With vat dyes, such as indigo, fabric is immersed in a dye bath and then removed and exposed to air or light, where the color change takes place. Vat dyes can be natural or synthetic, and usually require the addition of a reducing agent.	Acid dyes are specially formulated for protein fibers, and are great to use when trying to get a dark color on silk or wool. Although fiber-reactive dyes work on protein fibers as well, color shifts often occur and it is difficult to achieve deep colors or true black without acid dyes.	All purpose dyes, or grocery store dyes like Rit, are premixed and include direct dyes for cellulose, and acid dyes for protein and nylon. They are useful mainly for blended fabrics and not very permanent.	These can be used to create similar results as other dyes but in reverse. Because all fabrics are made up of different materials and dyes, the resulting color can sometimes be white or sometimes a pale-hued surprise. A bleach stop is necessary to deactivate the bleach at the end and render the effects permanent.
Difficult	Medium	Medium	Medium
All natural fibers	Protein fibers (wool, silk), nylon	Blended fabrics (wasteful for pure fibers)	Any natural or synthetic fiber
They don't fade in light, but color rubs off on skin and other fabrics.	Permanent	Not permanent; will wash out	Permanent
Cold-water method: immersion dye	Hot-water method: immersion dye in boiling water	Hot-water method: immersion dye in boiling water, or use in a washing machine	Cold-water methods: direct application (single color), immersion dye
Depends on the actual dye and additives used. Most are okay but others can be hazardous if inhaled, swallowed, or allowed to contact skin.	Protect eyes and lungs; dyes are safe when handled properly.	All-purpose dyes used to include known carcinogens. It is believed that they may have been phased out since the 1980s, but this is not certain because no ingredients are listed on the bottles.	Bleach gives off strong fumes and is an irritant, so always wear a mask and gloves and work in a well-ventilated area.

GLOSSARY

ADDITIVE Natural or chemical substance that can be used to assist dyes. Examples include urea, sodium alginate, calsolene oil, or even common household salt.

BAKING SODA A mild alkali that can be used instead of soda ash to help fiber-reactive dyes bond to fibers. It is weaker than soda ash and requires the assistance of heat.

BASE DYE Pure, unmixed dyes. These are colors with their own unique chemical makeup that are mixed together to create the hundreds of other hues available on the market. Different base dyes have their own characteristics and may react differently during the dye process.

BATIK A resist-dye method in which wax, mud, or paste is used to draw, stamp or print on fabric in the areas not to be dyed. After dyeing, it is removed and a design is left in relief.

BIND To tie or wrap the fabric in order to keep the dye from penetrating certain areas.

BLEACHING The process of removing color from fabric. Most tie-dye methods can be used with bleach to achieve a reverse effect.

BLEEDING The effect when dye runs and moves from the spot it was originally placed and either colors an undyed area or mixes with another color.

BLEND The mixture of two or more dye colors together. Also, a fabric made up of two or more different types of fibers.

BOND A permanent link between the dyes and the fibers.

BOTTLE DYEING A method of dyeing in which a concentrated dye mixture is applied directly to the garment using squeeze bottles.

CALSOLENE OIL An additive that helps break the surface tension of a dye bath and increase the evenness of the dye.

CELLULOSE FIBERS Fibers derived from plants, including cotton, linen, rayon, and hemp.

CHEMICAL WATER A blend of water and additives, dyes are added to it to create a direct application dye mixture.

COLD-WATER DYES Dyes that don't need to be heated to bond with fibers. This term is usually used in reference to fiber-reactive dyes, although other dyes exist that can be used in cold water as well.

COLORFAST The relative degree to which a fabric's color can withstand washing, weather, and exposure to light.

CONTRAST The degree to which colors are different from each other. This can refer to the hues themselves or to how light, dark, bright, or muted they are.

CURE The process of leaving dyes to bond with the fibers and become permanent.

DIP-DYE A method of dyeing fabric in which fabric is merely dipped part way into a dye bath. It can be a simple dipped line or a complicated ombré gradient.

DIRECT APPLICATION Any method of applying dye directly to fabric, including bottle dyeing, silk-screening, or hand painting.

DISCHARGE Any method of removing color from fabric, including bleaching.

DYE A natural or synthetic coloring agent that soaks into fabric and bonds with the fibers.

DYE BATH A mixture of dye, water, and additives used to soak fabric in for immersion dyeing.

EXHAUSTED DYE Dye that has used up all of its color potential so that it no longer dyes fabric, even if it still looks like it has color in it. This is a gradual process and dyes may become partially exhausted at first.

FIBER CONTENT The type or types of fibers that make up a fabric.

FIBER-REACTIVE DYES Versatile synthetic dyes used with natural fibers for the best colorfastness. They are used with cold water, which makes them the best dyes to use for tie-dye, batik, silk-screening, and fabric painting.

FIXATIVE/FIXER A chemical additive that helps the dye bond with the fiber.

HUE Color classified by it's most basic name. For example, red, green, blue, yellow.

IKAT A resist-dye method in which a design is marked out on threads that are tied and dyed in the design before being woven into fabric, creating a feathered effect.

IMMERSION DYEING A method of dyeing in which the fabric is soaked in a dye bath.

MONOCHROME A color palette consisting of just one hue, or color, in variations of value and saturation.

MORDANT A substance that helps a dye bond to fibers. With natural dyes, different mordants are used depending on the particular dye and the desired color.

NATURAL FIBERS Fibers made out of natural materials, including cellulose fibers such as cotton, linen, rayon, and hemp, and protein fibers such as silk and wool.

OMBRÉ Soft gradations of color, often achieved by raising fabric out of a dye bath slowly.

OVERDYEING A method of dyeing fabric that already has color, either solid or previously tie-dyed.

PH/PH LEVEL The level of acidity or alkalinity in a solution. For fiber-reactive dyes to bond with fabric, the fabric must be at the proper pH level, and soda ash is used to achieve this.

PRESOAK The process of soaking fabric in a solution of water and additives to prepare it to take the dye. We use soda ash for the presoak solution for fiber-reactive dyes.

PROCION DYES/PROCION MX DYE Brand name of fiber-reactive dyes.

PROTEIN FIBERS Fibers such as silk and wool derived from animal sources.

RELIEF The area that remains undyed in resist-dye methods such as tie-dye.

RESIST-DYE A dye method in which areas of the fabric are covered, tied, stitched, or folded to resist the application of dye, creating a pattern of undyed areas. Resist-dye methods include tie-dye, batik, and ikat.

SATURATION The level to which fabric has fully absorbed liquid or dye. Also, the level of intensity or purity in a color.

SET To allow the dye to bond with the fibers.

SHADE A darker version of a color, achieved by adding black.

SHIBORI The Japanese term for tie-dye.

SIZING A finish added to fabric or clothing to give it a specific quality, such as starch. Sizing interferes with the dye and should be washed off before dyeing the fabric.

SODA ASH A natural product, also known as sodium carbonate Na_2CO_3, it is a mild alkali that raises the pH level of fabric and allows fiber-reactive dyes to create a permanent bond with the fiber molecules.

SODIUM ALGINATE A natural additive made from seaweed that can be used to thicken dye.

SYNTHETIC DYE A dye that is derived from chemicals.

SYNTHETIC FIBERS Fibers that are chemically derived, such as polyester, nylon, acrylic, or spandex. Fiber-reactive dyes do not work on synthetic fibers.

SYNTHRAPOL A laundry detergent created to remove excess dye during the dyeing process.

TIE-DYE A resist-dye method in which fabric is tied, folded, stitched, or clamped to create a relief effect where the dye can't penetrate.

TINT A paler version of a color, achieved by diluting with water.

TONE A muted version of a color, achieved by adding gray or the color's complement.

TRITIK A tie-dye method in which fabric is stitched and pulled tight, leaving behind a design where the thread was sewn.

TRUE COLOR Accurate color results, as they are meant to appear.

UREA An additive used to help dissolve dyes more easily in water, and also to keep the fabric wet longer during the curing process.

WATER SOFTENER An additive used to treat hard water containing minerals that would otherwise interfere with the dyeing process.

RESOURCES

I like to support my local stores, so I always look locally before going to the big chains. Most of the items you need can be bought at your local mom-and-pop shops. And before doing that, check out your local thrift stores—or even your own closet—for materials and supplies.

ONE-STOP SHOPPING

DHARMA TRADING www.dharmatrading.com
The top tie-dye resource since 1969, Dharma Trading has great instructions on their website for all sorts of textile craft projects and sells everything you need to create those projects, including dyes, tools, chemicals; PFD clothing, home goods and fabrics; lots of how-to instructions, and some of the nicest people I've ever spoken to on the phone.

CLOTHING AND FABRIC

Tie-dye is a great way to give a second life to tired clothes, so hit up your local thrift stores and flea markets—and don't forget your own closet! Companies like Alternative Apparel and American Apparel make good blank cotton items, and fabric stores like Mood Designer Fabrics, B&J Fabrics, and Jo-Ann are great places to go if you want to make stuff from scratch.

TOOLS

Hardware stores, dollar stores, and kitchen supply stores can all be great places to find things like squeeze bottles, rubber bands, buckets, tarps, paintbrushes, and mixing supplies.

ONLINE RESOURCES

WWW.PBURCH.NET
Paula Burch is a scientist and dye enthusiast who has created a great forum for dye artists and novices alike to learn about and share dye discoveries.

WWW.SHIBORI.ORG
The World Shibori Network is dedicated to the preservation of Japanese *shibori* and similar tradtitional techniques across the globe. They hold an International Shibori Symposium every few years and maintain a website and blog.

DYES AND CHEMICALS

Fiber-reactive dyes and chemicals can be found at most arts and crafts stores. The dyes themselves come from a variety of manufacturers. The following companies all either sell dyes online or provide clear lists of retail stores in your area:

DHARMA TRADING www.dharmatrading.com
JACQUARD www.jacquardproducts.com
PROCHEM www.prochemicalanddye.com
GEORGE WEIL www.georgeweil.com
PATCHWORK SHOP www.patchworkshop.de
KRAFTCOLOR www.kraftkolour.net.au
DYLON www.dylon.co.uk

BOOKS

Brooklyn Makers: Food, Design, Craft, and Other Scenes from a Tactile Life by Jennifer Causey

Colors: What They Mean and How to Make Them by Anne Varichon

The Dyer's Art: Ikat, Batik, Plangi by Jack Lenor Larsen, Alfred Bühler Bronwen, and Garrett Solyon

Memory on Cloth: Shibori Now by Yoshiko Iwamoto Wada

Made by Hand by Lena Corwin

Shibori: The Inventive Art of Japanese Shaped Resist Dyeing by Yoshiko Iwamoto Wada, Mary Kellogg Rice, and Jane Barton

Shibori Recreated: A Place for Shibori in the 21st Century by Leah Rauch, Karen Davis, and Pepa Martin

Sight Unseen: Paper View by Monica Khemsurov and Jill Singer

Wild Color: The Complete Guide to Making and Using Natural Dyes by Jenny Dean

World Textiles: A Visual Guide by John Gillow and Bryan Sentance

PHOTO CREDITS

All still-life photography by Sarah Anne Ward.

All model and author photography by Paul Mpagi Sepuya.

Pages 8–9
Sarah Anne Ward Photography/Collection of the author.

Page 10
Ralph Koch Photography/Collection of Andres Moraga Textile Art.

Page 11
Robert Bengtson Photography/Collection of Thomas Murray.

Page 12
Don Tuttle Photography/Collection of Thomas Murray.

Page 13
Ralph Koch Photography/Collection of Andres Moraga Textile Art.

Page 14
(Top row, left to right)
Turban fragments, Jaipur, Rajasthan, India; leheria wrap-resist on cotton muslin, 19th century. Don Tuttle Photography/Collection of Steve and Gail Berger.

Futon cover, Japan; possible clamp-resist with indigo dye on cotton, 19th century. Robert Bengtson Photography/Collection of Thomas Murray.

Woman's shoulder cloth, Palambang, Sumatra; pelangi wrap-resist with synthetic dyes on silk, 19th century. Don Tuttle Photography/Collection of Thomas Murray.

(2nd row, left to right)
Agounoun ceremonial shoulder scarf, Berber (Aït Haddidou), Morocco; wrap-resist with synthetic dyes on wool, mid-20th century. Gebhart Blazek Photography/Collection of berber-arts.com.

Woman's veil, Berber, Atlas Mountains, Morocco; tie-dye with henna dye on wool, early 20th century. Don Tuttle Photography/Collection of Steve Berger and Thomas Murray.

Ndop ritual cloth, Bamileke, Cameroon; tritik stitch-resist with indigo dye on handspun cotton, early/mid-20th century. Don Tuttle Photography/Collection of Thomas Murray.

(3rd row, left to right)
Woman's dowry cloth (wrapper or shawl), Dioula, Ivory Coast; resist-dye on strip-woven cotton, mid-20th century. Ralph Koch Photography/Collection of Andres Moraga Textile Art.

Festival banner, Uzbek, Central Asia; wrap-resist with synthetic dyes on silk, early 20th century. Robert Bengtson Photography/Collection of Thomas Murray.

Taritat woman's ceremonial veil, Berber (Beni Ouarain), Morocco; wrap-resist with natural dyes and henna painted on wool muslin, mid-20th century. Gebhart Blazek Photography/Collection of berber-arts.com.

(4th row, left to right)
Lawon ritual shoulder cloth, Palambang, Sumatra, Indonesia; tritik stitch-resist with mixed dyes on silk, 19th/early 20th century. Don Tuttle Photography/Collection of Thomas Murray.

Ritual cloth, Dida, Ivory Coast; wrap-resist with natural dyes on raffia, 19th/early 20th century. Don Tuttle Photography/Collection of Thomas Murray.

Horse blanket, Tibet; wrap-resist with natural dyes on wool, 19th/early 20th century. Robert Bengtson Photography/Collection of Thomas Murray.

Page 15
(Top row, left to right)
Tadghart woman's ceremonial veil, Berber (Ida ou Zeddoute), Morocco; tie-dye with natural dyes on wool, early 20th century. Don Tuttle Photography/Collection of Thomas Murray.

Mosen tea ceremony cloth, Mongolia, for the Japanese market; wrap-resist on wool felt, 19th century. Robert Bengtson Photography/Collection of Thomas Murray.

Ukara cloth, Igbo, Nigeria; tie-dye with indigo dye on handspun cotton, early 20th century. Don Tuttle Photography/Collection of Thomas Murray.

(2nd row, left to right)
Ukara cloth, Igbo, Nigeria; tie-dye with indigo dye on handspun cotton, early 20th century. Robert Bengtson Photography/Collection of Thomas Murray.

Man's ceremonial skirt, Kuba, Kasai Province, DR Congo; bound and stick-stitch-clamp resist with tannic and mud dyes on raffia, 20th century. Don Tuttle Photography/Collection of Andres Moraga Textile Art.

Banner, Bali/Lombopk, Indonesia; tritik stitch-resist and pelangi wrap-resist with synthetic dyes on silk, early 20th century. Don Tuttle Photography/Collection of Thomas Murray.

(3rd row, left to right)
Mantle, Nazca culture, Peru; wrap-resist with natural dyes on camelid hair, 400–600 AD. Don Tuttle Photography/Courtesy of Steve and Gail Berger.

Futon cover, Japan; shibori wrap-resist with indigo dye on cotton, 19th/early 20th century. Robert Bengtson Photography/Collection of Thomas Murray.

Ritual emblem of a chief, Dida, Ivory Coast; stitch-resist with natural dyes on raffia, 19th/early 20th century. Don Tuttle Photography/Collection of Thomas Murray.

(4th row, left to right)
Woman's summer kimono, Japan; shibori clamp-resist with indigo dye on cotton, 19th/early 20th century. Robert Bengtson Photography/Collection of Thomas Murray.

Agounoun scarf, Berber, Morocco; tie-dye with natural dyes on wool, 19th/early 20th century. Don Tuttle Photography/Collection of Steve Berger and Thomas Murray.

Mendil head shawl, Berber, Tunisia; wrap-resist with mixed dyes on wool, early 20th century. Don Tuttle Photography/Collection of Thomas Murray.

Page 16
Huari piecework tunic, Huari culture, Peru; amarra wrap-resist with natural dyes on camelid hair, 750–950 AD. Collection of The Textile Museum 91.341, acquired by George Hewitt Myers in 1941.

ACKNOWLEDGMENTS

Thank you to all of my friends, family, clients, and students for your inspiration, encouragement and support. Thank you JoJo Li, Lydia Turner, Sarah Anne Ward, Paul Mpagi Sepuya, and Lydia Stone for making this book a true work of art, and a special thanks to JoJo, Lydia, and Anna Wolfgang for being true friends, amazing collaborators, and for your constant inspiration in my life and work.

Thank you to my family, Shauna Simon, Stefan Alexander, Zach Simon-Alexander, and Devi Kirn, for your unconditional love and support, for being my biggest fans, and for being the most colorful family around.

Thank you to all of the special women who have helped out in the studio and on development of the book, especially Kirsten Garrison, Meredith Goldstein, Eviana Hartman, Mabel Ogawa, Cynthia Vanis, and Natasha Vora, for sharing in this exciting process with me.

Thank you to Dani Griffiths for modeling for this book and gracing it with your beauty.

Thank you to Chris Oh for painting the amazing mural featured in the author photo.

Thank you to all of the textile collectors and scholars who so generously and enthusiastically shared their passion, knowledge, and beautiful images, especially Gebhart Blazek, Steve and Gail Berger, Andrew Hale, Andres Moraga and Vanessa Drake Moraga, and Thomas Murray.

Thank you to the unnamed woman in the garden who gave me my first tie-dye tutorial, and to Ivy at Dharma Trading for trouble-shooting with me over the phone all these years with such enthusiasm. Thank you to Lena Corwin for encouraging me to share and write and educate, and to the Textile Arts Center for giving me a home to teach. Thank you to Betty Wong, my editor, for envisioning this book.

Thank you, Antoine Catala, whom I love.

And thank you, for reading this book and sharing my passion. I hope you have fun and I'm so excited to see what you create. If you'd like to share your creations, please send photos to shareit@shabdismyname.com.

ABOUT THE AUTHOR

SHABD SIMON-ALEXANDER is an internationally renowned dye artist with a background in fine arts. Her clothing line, *shabd*, is carried in high-end boutiques and contemporary art museums around the world. She teaches hand-dyeing and had the honor of teaching Martha Stewart how to tie-dye. She lives in New York City. For more information about Shabd, visit her at www.shabdismyname.com

INDEX